OZARK WRITERS ON WRITING

Essays on Creativity

OZARK WRITERS ON WRITING

Essays on Creativity

Edited by L. Pate

Seven Oaks Publishing Company
Conway, Arkansas

Published by Seven Oaks Publishing Company
P.O. Box 1103, Conway, Arkansas 72033

Printed in the United States of America

10 9 8 7 6 5 4 3 2 1

Library of Congress Catalog Card Number: 95-71608

ISBN 0-9630829-4-9

First Edition, 1995

Project Director and Editor: L. Pate

SEVEN OAKS PUBLISHING COMPANY
CONWAY, ARKANSAS

CONTENTS

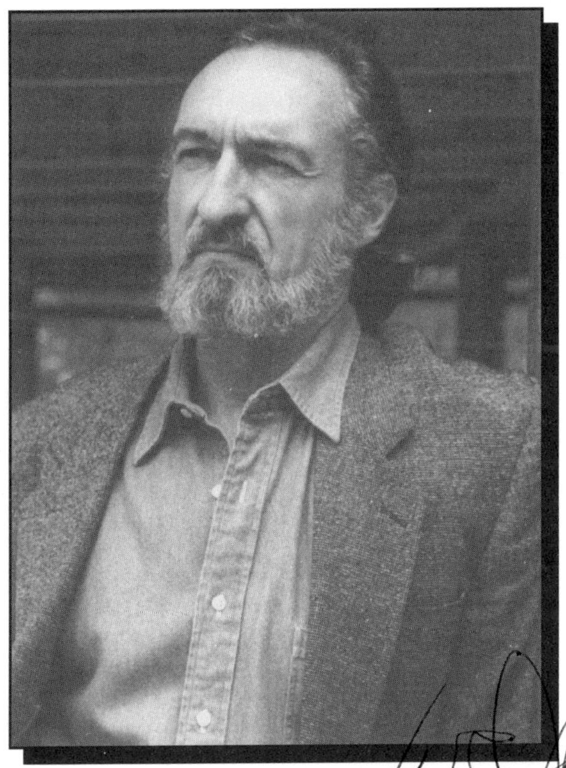

W.C. Jameson

Award-winning newspaper columnist W.C. Jameson is the author of 200 magazine articles and eighteen books, including the popular Buried Treasures of America Series. His book *A Sense of Place: Essays on the Ozarks* is currently in its second printing.

He is a professional musician and poet and is a former field editor for two national magazines.

Jameson resides in Conway, Arkansas, with his wife, Tonya, and their left-handed Labrador Retriever, Gus. He relaxes by searching for lost mines and buried treasure, riding his motorcycle, and trout fishing with his sons.

INTRODUCTION

Mining Literary Gold in the Ozarks

Ever since the publishing industry became a viable and important enterprise in America, a variety of different geographic regions have waxed and waned relative to prominence as sources of important writers and writing, to receiving critical attention, and to achieving notice among the nation's major publishers.

In the 1980s, James Ward Lee said, "In the United States, there are three distinct regional literary traditions – the South, California, and Texas."

For a time, Southern literature was all the rage, and the reading public couldn't get enough of the likes of Faulkner, Welty, O'Connor, and other influential and appealing Southern authors. Following a period of being generally ignored by New York-based publishers and critics during much of the 1960s, 1970s, and early 1980s, the South is currently experiencing a vigorous renaissance in writing and publication. The growing popularity of the South, Southern culture, and Southern writers and writing, has resulted in important book sales and in attracting the attention of more and more publishers as well as the reading public. From a literary standpoint, the South is clearly on the rise once again.

During the 1970s and 1980s, Texas literature and Texas writers caught and held the attention of major publishers, critics, and readers, and the works of Texas authors Larry McMurtry, Larry L. King, Elmer Kelton, and others were in demand among American readers. Today, the positive momentum associated with Texas writers and writers is continuing.

In recent years, the book-buying public has also seen an impressive growth of a significant body of literature from the geographic regions of the Pacific Northwest, California, the Great Plains, and the Mid-West.

Currently making some impressive inroads and gaining ground on the current regional favorites are the Ozark Mountains, a heretofore virtually ignored, unsung, and, for the most part, relatively unnoticed environment normally associated with moonshine stills, Li'l Abner, bumpkins, barefootedness, and backwardness.

While most of the country's population has been occupied with the distractions of day to day living, the geographic realm that is the Ozark Mountains was undergoing dramatic population growth and now serves as setting for several important cities. Ozark writers, quietly increasing in numbers, are crafting and polishing their works in the relative solitude and splendor of these gentle mountains and gaining notice from a number of important national, regional, and university publishers. In recent years, an impressive array of novels, biographies, non-fiction, and folklore, all with Ozark connections, have been released by major publishing companies. Ozark characters and settings are achieving a ubiquity never before experienced, and Ozark writers, poets, and storytellers are receiving increasing shelf space in bookstores and libraries around the country and the world.

Scholars ask, "Is there a body of literature one can call Ozark? Is there such a thing as an Ozark Literature? An Ozark writer? What is the difference between an Ozark writer, a regional writer, and a provincial writer?"

The growing literary tradition in the Ozarks is considerably younger than those of the South and Texas, and as with anything new, only time will provide the answers. For the time being, however, there are some common threads that run through the works of Ozark writers.

Principal adhesives that binds Ozark writers are a clear and profound sense of place and an ability to capture the essence of the environment and its residents from frontier times to the present. This acute sense of place is manifested in novels, essays, poetry, nonfiction works, newspaper columns, and storytelling.

Some may argue that a sense of place is also powerfully communicated by Southern and Texas writers, and that cannot be denied, but where Southerners and Texans may elevate place to the near-importance of a character in some cases, the role of place in the Ozark realm is more often than not one of a shaper, an influential companion, a subtle and silent advisor or friend, a hearth.

The Physical Setting

The Ozark Mountains are found in all or part of ninety-three counties in the states of Arkansas, Kansas, Missouri, and Oklahoma, and they cover approximately fifty thousand square miles.

This thick and layered formation was alternately submerged beneath prehistoric seas and uplifted to higher altitudes several times during the past four hundred million years. With the passage of more time, the range ultimately reached its current climax condition and now serves as a stage for a variety of life and landscape that exist nowhere else in the world.

The Ozark Mountains are rich in resources, but not necessarily the kind most people normally associate with the rocks and landscape of the earth. Although persistent entrepreneurs mine from the Ozark bedrock a variety of minerals, the region, in all likelihood, provides a richer resource in the form of literary potential.

Rocks and minerals such as quartz, bentonite, phosphate, and gas, along with some sand and gravel, are extracted from the Ozark limestone. In the not too distant past, the mining of lead and zinc were viable industries here, and over four centuries ago, according to legend, Spanish explorers under the leadership of Hernando DeSoto discovered and mined quantities of gold and silver from the region.

Today, however, the Ozark Mountains serve as a special setting and source for a different kind of resource, one that may ultimately prove to be richer than the Spanish gold. Within the boundaries of this unique mountain range lies a virtually untapped literary treasure as it relates to real and potential topics, settings, characters, and the writers who turn them into books and articles. Literally dozens of authors, poets, storytellers, newspaper columnists, artists, and photographers are currently involved in mining the belletristic potential of the Ozark Mountains, but they have only scratched the surface.

The Cultural Setting

What makes the Ozarks so rich in this kind of potential? What makes this region different from other geographic areas? What makes it special from a literary and artistic standpoint?

The answer to those questions may ultimately lie in the mix and variety of the cultures that moved into, settled, passed through, and ultimately influenced this region.

The Indian tribes that migrated into the Ozark range developed, over the generations, their own unique folkways, religion, music, storytelling, and other traditions. Later immigrant cultures, the Europeans and their descendants, who subsequently moved into the Ozarks to make their living and establish communities, often brought with them a kind of cultural baggage that included a different set of folkways, their own unique music, lore, traditions, tales, and legends.

For centuries, long before the arrival of the Spanish explorers, a number of different Indian tribes lived in the Ozark Mountains. These sons and daughters of the land evolved a way of life and a manner of living in harmony with the sometimes harsh environment. In many ways, the land served to shape their perceptions, their ideals and religions, and provided the settings, characters, and animals for many of their myths and legends.

During the early 1500s, the Spaniards under the leadership of DeSoto arrived to explore, conquer, convert, and extract whatever riches from the earth they could find. There was inevitable interaction between the Indians and the Spanish invaders, interaction that often resulted in warfare, but other times in trade and friendship. Though the Spaniards eventually departed, legend claims that some remained in the region, intermarried with the Indians, and became assimilated into the native culture. Spanish place names are not uncommon throughout the Ozarks.

Late in the seventeenth century, French explorers, trappers, hunters, traders, and entrepreneurs arrived in the Ozarks and saw promise and potential in the grand limestone hills and valleys. These newcomers and their ways mixed with those of the natives, uneasily at first, but eventually with harmony.

French control of the region lasted until 1764, at which time Spanish rule was reestablished and maintained off and on until 1804. Gradually, the dark and mysterious Ozarks were slowly opened up to others who responded to information carried eastward, information about opportunities related to trapping, hunting, and farming in this area. Slowly, at first, white settlers began to trickle in. Some were originally bound for the western prairies and plains and decided to remain. Others simply came into the region in search of a better life and a chance to claim land for their own. Many of these folk landed in parts of the Ozarks. In time, more and more Upper and Lower South Anglos began arriving from Kentucky, Tennessee, Alabama, Georgia, Mississippi, and the Carolinas. One by one, family by family, they filtered into the Ozarks and established small communities, most of them quite isolated and remote.

These new residents entered a relatively primitive wilderness that offered little in the way of amenities. While breaking the thin, rocky soils in preparation for cultivation and cutting logs for dwellings, they often had to hunt wild game in the dense woodlands to provide food. In this remote and isolated land, the settlers were forced to serve as their own doctors and teachers while they learned how to survive. Like those that came before them, they brought their own unique folkways, practices, and beliefs. In addition, they were introduced to the ways of the area Indians, and there followed an inevitable sharing of knowledge, and even more was accumulated from subsequent experience.

The traditions and practices employed by Indians and whites alike were subsequently handed down from parent to offspring in the oral tradition, a strong and important source of history, lore, and legend. Even today, many scholars maintain much of the important history and lore of the Ozarks exists not on paper and in books, but in the minds and memories of the old-timers who carved out a living in this land.

The lore, the legends, the stories, the traditions, the folkways, the foodways, the folk cures, and the folk wisdom remain a strong and important aspect of Ozark culture, whether Anglo, Indian, Spanish, or other. Tales of the past, of ghosts, spirits, animals, unknown creatures, lost mines, and buried treasures were kept alive orally over the generations in this remote and relatively isolated mountain range, and here the stories, the tales, remained unadulterated from outside influence.

Population growth in the Ozarks increased gradually following the Civil War as more and more people discovered the potential in poultry farming and settlement. Towns and cities grew, slowly at first, and later with a vigor heretofore unseen in what was only recently a wilderness. More and more schools dotted the landscape, and as formal education gained a foothold and the citizens were exposed to the writing and poetry of others, literary seeds were planted in the minds of the young. The intellectual bounty of the Ozark Mountains was taking root, and needed only to be nurtured.

Though the region abounded in clear streams, fresh water springs, clean air, and abundant game, the limestone bedrock yielded only a thin and relatively poor soil. Initially, coaxing crops from the ground required a heavy investment of time and labor, leaving the residents precious little time for anything else such as reading and writing.

In many ways the people who made the Ozarks their home were like the soil – undeveloped, yet with potential. This condition resulted from simple lack of opportunity and being forced to carve an existence, a livelihood, out of the sometimes grudging land. Because of the formidable burden of providing for a living, the people had few, if any, opportunities to stretch their creative muscles, to read, to write.

In spite of the hardships facing these pioneers, there existed among them a few who began recording the ways of the folk. Many of the stories and legends and much of the lore were written down for the first time, as were interpretations of historical events. Journals and diaries were kept and maintained, providing insight into the life of generations ago. From these early efforts the germination of a literary tradition began to grow.

The Ozarks, Writers, and Writing

Pertinent changes in the contributions to and the perceptions of Ozark writing began occurring around the beginning of the twentieth century. The seeds of literary tradition, firmly planted in the region, began germinating and were manifested in the form of published works that attracted some notice around the country.

Arguably, the earliest Ozark work that could be credited for generating some attention to the region was Harold Bell Wright's *The Shepherd of the Hills*, published in 1907. *Shepherd*, which is still in print, introduced many Americans to the Ozark Mountains and its people.

Other notable early creations emanating from the Ozarks during the first half of the twentieth century included Charles J. Finger's *Ozark Fantasia* (1926), Wayman Hogue's *Back Yonder: An Ozark Chronicle* (1931), Fred W. Allsopp's two volumes of *Folklore of Romantic Arkansas* (1931). Vance Randolph, along with Allsopp, encountered a treasure trove of folklore in the Ozark environs, folklore long communicated between the people, the cultures. For forty years, Randolph collected the folklore and folkways of

Ozarkers and saw the publication of dozens of his books, many by prestigious publishing houses.

Other noted Ozark writers of the first half of the twentieth century included: Otto Ernest Rayburn, considered to be one of the most important writers and speakers on Ozark folkways during the 1920s and 1930s; Thomas Hart Benton, the famous painter who often wrote about the Ozarks; Fred Starr, who contributed several books of essays during the fifties and sixties.

It has only been in the last thirty to forty years that Ozark writers and Ozark settings have made truly significant inroads into the generally conservative literary world and gained recognition among their peers throughout the country. In the process, they have caught the attention of the New York publishers.

Among the more prominent contemporary writers with strong Ozark connections are Douglas C. Jones, Donald Harrington, Joan Hess, Jory Sherman, Max McCoy, and Robert Conley. Each are distinguished in their use of Ozark settings and characters and in their communication of a sense of place that is typically regional.

Arkansas native Douglas C. Jones is the author of a number of wonderful books including *The Court-Marital of George Armstrong Custer*, *Gone the Dreams and Dancing*, and *Remember Santiago*. A two-time winner of the prestigious Western Writers of America Spur Award as well as the recipient of the Owen Wister Award for lifetime achievement, Jones is a member of Who's Who in America. Author Jones has successfully employed Ozark settings and strong regional characters in several books including *Winding Stair*, *Elkhorn Tavern*, *The Barefoot Brigade*, *Come Winter*, and *The Search For Temperance Moon*. In reading Jones' works, one easily discerns a distinct passion for the Ozarks and a fine ear for the regional dialect. Jones' love for the land, its history, and its people is evident, and after reading one of his Ozark-based historical novels, one comes away with an intimacy and feeling for the region and its residents rarely captured by any other writer. With his books, Jones has single-handedly introduced the Ozarks to tens of thousands of readers.

Spur Award winner Jory Sherman, author of over 150 books, has lived in the Ozarks for over two decades. After residing in many different locations in this country and others, Sherman fell in love with the Ozark Mountains from the moment he arrived and felt a kind of kinship and spirit here encountered nowhere else. Sherman decided to remain, and over the years a number of his writings have featured Ozark settings and characters. Two of his books of essays, *My Heart is in the Ozarks* and *An Early Frost*, are among the finest collections of pieces on Ozark people, places, and things ever written.

Max McCoy, award winning author and a native of southeastern Kansas on the periphery of the Ozark Mountains, is another author who has a keen sense of place, and incorporates regional elements into his novels with an enviable skill.

Other notable Ozark writers who have so expertly and sensitively captured the spirit of place in their works include Velda Brotherton, Ellen Gray Massey, and Charlotte Sherman. They are all writers who have successfully mined the culture and settings of the Ozark Mountains, incorporated them into their works, and offered them for others to enjoy and delight in. Their books contain a strong sense of place which they easily, and proudly, communicate to the reader.

Like authors, a number of poets have responded to the Ozark inspirations with well-received and oft-recognized creations. Two volumes of poetry by Otto Ernest Rayburn are believed by many to be the first to be closely associated with this grand mountain range. Joplin, Missouri's, Langston Hughes, another important poet, never forgot his Ozark roots.

In more contemporary times, prominent poets with strong Ozark connections have included C.D. Wright, Frank Stanford, Miller Williams, Robert Dyer, and Jack Butler. Each has earned the recognition and praise of contemporaries around the nation.

Songwriter Jimmy Driftwood, a native of Stone County, Arkansas, often captured important images of the Ozark residents and special places in many of his published songs. Driftwood, a three-time Grammy Award winner, wrote *The Battle of New Orleans* and *Tennessee Stud,* and was the driving force behind the establishment of the Ozark Folk Center. He is still performing and writing in his mid-eighties.

The oral tradition, the source of so many tales and inspirations, is alive and well in the Ozark Mountains, and is manifested best in the renderings of master storytellers Richard and Judy Dockery Young. Professional storytellers who have authored several books, the Youngs perform regularly throughout the region and perpetuate an important component of Ozark literature.

Today and the Future

More and better writers are emerging from the Ozarks with astonishing regularity, their works becoming recognized across a wide spectrum of literature and region.

In addition, new publishing companies located in and near the Ozarks that publish Ozark-related material are reporting growing successes, and offer excellent opportunites for regional writers. These presses have produced some important books that likely would never have been considered by major New York publishers because of the specific regional, and thus somewhat esoteric, flavor. A number of

Ozark writers first gained recognition and success with regional presses before being signed to contracts with major publishing firms.

A growing number of excellent writers conferences in the Ozarks have served as important gatherings for professionals as well as novices and provide formats in which to discuss writing, agenting, poetry, and the market place.

The famous Ozark Creative Writers Conference, held each October in Eureka Springs, Arkansas, has gained a national reputation as being one of the finest regional gatherings of writers in the country. It features noted authors, editors, agents, and poets who lecture and conduct workshops.

The Ozark Writers League, which holds a day-long conference four times each year in Hollister, Missouri, has produced consistently excellent programs. The Missouri Writers Guild holds an annual conference in a different location in that state each year. Lying just outside the boundary of the Ozarks in southeastern Missouri, The Heartland Writers Guild sponsors a three-day conference that attracts published authors as well as beginning writers from across mid-America.

During the Ozark Creative Writers conference in 1995, it was learned that several New York publishers are growing increasingly interested in Ozark-related material, specifically fiction which contains Ozark characters and Ozark settings. The source of this insight, a literary agent, suggests that the Ozarks are becoming one of the favored regions among the American reading public.

This makes sense, for despite the successes of Ozarkers Douglas C. Jones, Joan Hess, Jory Sherman, and others, the growing literary resources found in this special region are only just now beginning to be tapped. At this writing, there exists a bounty of Ozark-inspired settings, topics, and characters that appear never-ending.

For non-fiction writers, a deep and wide gap currently exists in the research and writing of Ozark history, biography, and folklore. Despite the numerous contributions of Vance Randolph and others, there remains a great deal of research and writing to be done on an unlimited variety of Ozark folklore including tales of ghosts and hauntings, Indian lore and mysteries, foodways, folk sayings, folk medicine, fishing stories, music, tales of lost mines and buried treasures, outlaw tales, animal tales, and more. These resources appear endless, and are simply waiting for energetic and enthusiastic writers to begin mining.

* * *

Ozark Writers on Writing is a book by writers closely linked to the Ozark Mountain by birthright, choice, or by virtue of their contributions, observations, insights, or opinions. As the literary tradition of Ozark realm matures, it is anticipated that more and more talented writers from the region will begin receiving important recognition, critical acclaim, and publishing success. As that occurs, additional chapters will need to be added to this volume in order to ensure that their insights and observations can be made available to readers.

For now, it is becoming easier than ever to look upon the literary sons and daughters of the Ozark realm with pride as the regional successes are counted and as the contributions to America's body of writing are considered. In the pages that follow, ten prominent Ozark writers share some of their insights, experiences, and observations. In large part, it is they who have helped thrust the region into national prominence and acceptance.

The future of Ozarks literature and Ozarks writers looks bright and promising.

And it's about time.

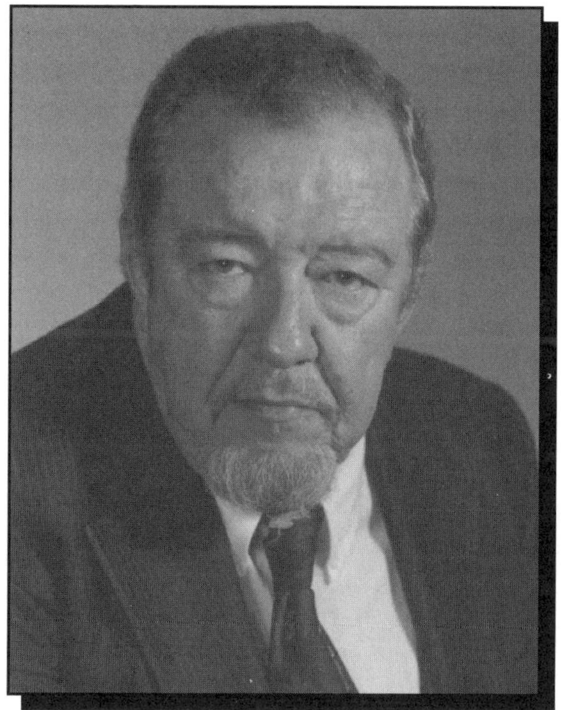

Douglas C. Jones

Multi-award winning author Doug Jones has written seventeen books and numerous articles in historical and journalism periodicals. He is also an accomplished artist with shows held in Washington, D.C., Madison, WI, Tulsa, OK, and Fayetteville, AR.

His 1976 novel *The Court Marshal of George Armstrong Custer* won the Western Writers of America Spur Award for Best Novel of the West. It was later made into a Hallmark Hall of Fame television movie.

He is a member of Who's Who in America and in 1993 was awarded the Owen Wister Award for Lifetime Achievement by the Western Writers of America.

Jones was born in Winslow, Arkansas, and currently resides in Fayetteville, Arkansas with his wife, Mary.

The Old Breed

Now, in these waning years of the 20th Century, it has become fashionable for writers to come, singing praises of the wonderful Ozark hills in stimulating the creative juices. Come to the mountains like flocks of winter starlings, foreign to the environment, yet chirping and warbling and hopping about as they publish many and varied things, attributing inspiration to the locale.

These wonderful folds of tree-covered mountains, they say. The clear flowing water, the lakes, the friendly folk, the mystic ambrosia rising from the underlying sacred limestone, they say.

For a long time, that missed me. For a long time I reckoned I could write Arkansas stories about hill people as I sat in a New York City loft or in a Leavenworth barracks.

For seventy years, it had been just a place where you play sandlot baseball. A place where spring tree frogs told you when you could sleep with your windows open. For seventy years, I thought it was just the normal burst of red and orange and yellow in the trees along every slope in October. For seventy years, I thought it was natural, not anything unusual. Not anything inspirational, anyway.

Therefore, when I came back to the Ozarks after

almost thirty years dwelling in other places, I was doing nothing more than coming home. To where I started.

And began to write. As I had planned to do, no matter where I touched down after retiring from other things.

But maybe the flatlanders heard some music I'd missed because all along I'd been too close to the tambourines. Looking back, it's pretty obvious that there was something around here that encouraged storytelling.

The Old Folks, most of whom the newcomer writers never saw, were storytellers. Tough, freedom-loving, sure-shot, singing, dancing, individualists who mistrusted most strangers and all government. Hence, laconic. But whom among themselves were not only garrulous but extraordinary raconteurs.

Many were barely literate, but they sure as hell could spin the stories that, taken together, spelled out life and death and who they were and where they came from and when you might expect rain.

And the best of these were not tall tales, but like much legend, had a solid basis in fact. It was what the Osage might call oral history. Spun out by an old man or woman to reflect the joy and sadness of the tribe in coming to where they were.

Take Old Bill. Old Bill was a blue roan Grandfather rode to deliver the mail, Grandfather being a rural letter carrier on a route that started in Winslow, Arkansas, and extended in a loop westward through wild woods and mountains.

Sometimes, when Grandfather got home early, he'd let me ride Old Bill from the road in front of Grandmother's house to the barn up the hill behind. Old Bill was a gentle gelding. And a talking horse, too.

Grandfather explained it. When he was mail carrier, riding that wild country and met another rider, Grandfather would rein Old Bill around broadside to the approaching horseman so he could talk without having to raise himself in the stirrups in order to see over Old Bill's ears.

Soon, Old Bill understood this so as soon as he saw another rider coming, he would stop and turn himself broadside in the road so Grandfather could talk a while.

It came to pass, as they say, that one day Grandfather was crossing a ford about four miles from town, heading home. There was a deep cut in the creek banks here where the road crossed and Old Bill had waded the stream and was in the cut when two men appeared on horseback coming from the direction of Winslow.

> They were in a considerable hurry, Grandfather said. But as soon as Old Bill saw them, he turned broadside right there in the cut. Which blocked the road.
>
> There was a lot of gravel and dirt flying around when they pulled on the reins to keep from running into Old Bill. They were armed. I saw pistols and a shotgun in a saddle boot. But nothing unusual about that, out in the tall timber. They were young, handsome men. I didn't know either one of them, but they knew me.
>
> They both laughed and one of them said, "Looks like you got a talkin horse there, Mr. Stockburger."
>
> I got Old Bill out of the way and they reined around us and went off towards Oklahoma kicking up a lot of spray crossing the ford. Then me and Bill rode on towards town. In about five minutes, we met the posse. Those two nice boys had robbed the bank in Winslow. Well, Old Bill sensed the crime. When the posse come at us, he didn't even turn broadside so I could talk.

They never caught those guys. They never caught anybody who robbed the Winslow bank, which happened periodically. In fact, a lot of people claimed they had a bank in Winslow just so guys who didn't have anything else to do would have something to rob.

I saw one. A long time ago. Before most people in the hills had ever seen their first airplane or black man or cotton candy. I'm not sure if I really remember or if what I remember is what Grandmother told me I remembered.

> I was in the rocker by that window where I could look right down into town, where the bank was at, Grandmother said. I had a dish pan of sting beans in my lap, breaking them to cook for supper. Something looked mighty suspicious at the bank.

Sure enough, while we watched, four men ran out of the bank and got on horses. That's right. *Horses*. And rode up west mountain and I guess out toward Devil's Den and on to Oklahoma. After a while, Grandmother went to the hand-crank telephone on the wall and called the Central Office.

> Miss Lyda said it was true. They'd robbed the bank and she expected the Sheriff at Fayetteville was going to leave his card game at the jail long enough to come down and take a look-see.

They never caught those guys, either.

Listen, Grandmother may have helped my memory on that robbery, but she was a fair-to-middlin tale spinner in her own right and it's hard for me to say how many of her stories have turned up in my own perception of local history.

> Our people came in wagons with Bibles and flintlock muskets and established Shilo Church, my Grandmother said. And now it's a town and some of your great aunts live there and when they came, there were bears in the timbers and Osage hunting parties! They make good gooseberry pies, too. Your aunts. Not the Osage.

Can you imagine the chill going up the back of a seven-year-old child, listening to that? Osage hunting parties! Right there in the woods where you've gone to collect mushrooms.

> Mother Quinton told me, Grandmother said. They'd come and steal everything you had and scrap the dirt off the smoke house floor for the salt. All the men were gone. In an army someplace or in one of those jake-leg bandit bands we had around here after the armies fought and then left to fight somewheres else.

She wasn't talking about Osage or Cherokee then. She was talking about men banded together with the Civil War as an excuse to pillage and steal and murder. Red-leg, bushwhacker, night rider, partisan marauder. Barn burning in the night. And many women alone, I suspect counting out the hours, tense to the sounds of darkness.

> I guess it was after that battle at Elkhorn Tavern. Mother Quinton was at the Benton County farm with four family women. No men, they was off fightin somewheres.
>
> One night they heard this call from the dark. Like a new baby cryin. They was all in nightgowns, ready for sleep, but Mother Quinton taken a shotgun and a lantern and went out with all the girls taggin along and they found this Yankee soldier boy gutted like a slaughter yard hog and put him in a blanket and dragged him up to the house but he died before they could get him inside.
>
> They taken a garnet ring off his finger and they taken his boots and they wrapped him in the blanket and dragged him back to the fence corner behind the chicken coop where they found him, and they buried him.

Two years later an old couple came from Cassville, Missouri, and identified the ring and had the body dug up and taken home. They'd been traveling all round trying to find their son, who had been an officer in the Union Army of Southwest Missouri.

> Your Grandfather's people fought for the South. My family had men on both sides. My daddy was a sergeant in the Union army, Grandmother said. Wounded. Battle of Wilson Creek and give a pension all the rest of his life. He lived in Indian Territory and so his brother raised me and was my daddy, I guess. And I always called my real daddy Uncle Jeff because his name was Jefferson Quinton and sometimes he'd come from the Indian Nations and bring me some lemon drop candy. He had a medal. He was a hero, I reckon.

And just as sacred, the running dogs of the night. Oh yes, they were running dogs and they ran at night, after the fox in those wooded hills, long legged, white and brown and orange and black, tongue as long as buggy whips and in the sun lazy dusty sleepy but with dusk brown eyes going sharp and tongues rose red and bodies ready to lance the night and voices bell-like, quavering so delicately it made the stars blink! Well, I always thought it made the stars blink. On some dark ridge with the hickory and oak and red gum close around, listening to Grandfather tell stories, and listening to the dogs running a fox along a ridge barely within hearing. Damn right! The stars blinked!

"Dixie was the best fox dog God ever created," Grandfather said. Throat like silver trumpets echoing through those hills. I heard Dixie hard after a fox many times. She had a voice tuned only for that tall timber. It sounded on many moon-lit nights. Until she was run over by a car on the new cement ribbon called US 71, a thing you would not expect a simple fox hound to understand.

Grandfather said there was no comparison between that dog's keening and the roar of automobiles along the hard surface strip, and no stink of gasoline, either.

An inordinate number of those stories were violent or fed on some kind of violence. Well, it was a violent place, along the old Indian Nations border. We almost took it for granted. But never, as a child, were we afraid somebody was going to ride past the house and shoot us. Shooting at each other was for grown-ups.

Sometimes we got involved though. Like Aunt Glenn told the story.

> It was early '30's. One night Mr. Vandiver, the town constable, came up to the house and borrowed Papa's pistol. Mr. Vandiver said there might be some trouble in town.

It was a little Colt double action .38. Grandfather had bought it years before to carry on the mail route, in case he saw a red wolf or a big timber rattlesnake.

Anyway, this gully-washer storm blew in from Oklahoma. The earth shook and quivered with thunder and the lightening flashed and the noise was hard to imagine. Right in the middle of all this, I got a long, rotten-wood pine splinter in the bottom of my bare foot running on the back porch. The women took over. There was Grandmother, Mother, Aunt Hazel and Aunt Glenn. They dragged me kicking and screaming to the emergency room, which in every hill country house was the kitchen. They lay me out on the kitchen table, me still kicking and screaming. The chief surgeon was Grandmother. She had a bottle of rubbing alcohol and tweezers, and the instrument that induced all the kicking and screaming. A straight razor. She hadn't used it yet, but I knew she was about to.

While Mama went after the splinter, Aunt Glenn said, His mother held one leg, Hazel held the other, and I held the top of him and it was my job to console him with the news we'd just had from the tie yard down town.

Aunt Glenn said I was lucky. What if you was that man down in the tie yard, lying in the rain, because Mr. Vandiver shot him with Papa's pistol. It *really* hurts that man, getting shot with Papa's pistol, and all you've got is just a little bitty splinter.

Little bitty! Hell, it was an axe handle and my own people were going to slice my foot to get it out. I hated all of them! Until they got the splinter out. Then I tried to imagine that man in the tie yard, shot with Grandfather's pistol.

"And layin in the rain, too," my little sister said.

"Go jump off a rock!" I said, not needing anybody to help me visualize bloody scenes.

I sure enough didn't need help in visualizing such things a few weeks later when Grandfather was driving out to this hill farm where a man was keeping Grandfather's fox dogs. My sisters and I were with him. And we came to this terrible car wreck, and mangled machines were on the shoulders and people were standing around waiting for the state cops to arrive and right in the middle on the concrete slab was a dead man, twisted and red and horrible and of course, my sisters and I were trying to see everything about him there was to see.

As Grandfather eased the car past the man, he said, "Don't look at him. He wouldn't want you to see him like that."

Over the next thirty years, in the army, three wars, urban riots, training accidents, there were a lot of dead men. I never looked at one without remembering what Grandfather said that day.

And when you're writing, that kind of thing can't be kept out. And you don't want it to be kept out because it's real. If it's destructive to what you're trying to say, you write around it, you avoid it. But if it helps the mood, the theme or the characterization, you emphasize it.

Don't ask me how. But after the fact, after the words are written, those background tunes are there and they come from some deep well of experience that you take to sleep every night. If you don't hear that faint music, if you have never written a sentence that sings to you, a small collection of words that makes the hair stand up on the back of your neck, you're in pursuit of the wrong goal. Find another Golden Fleece.

This isn't to say you've got to have experienced everything you write. You go into the past and into other worlds by reading, mostly, but when you write about it, those life experiences of your own have got to flavor it, like the sage in the sausage.

And listening, too. That's as good as reading when it comes to putting you in another place and time.

A couple of years before the Great Depression broke out, there were still a lot of old guys in Ft. Smith, Arkansas, who had been peace officers of one kind or another back in the days of the Parker court. That Federal Court with jurisdiction in the Indian Territory. These men usually hung out around the jail and courthouse and the various automobile agencies. My father traded old pistols with them and listened to their stories and came home and told those stories about the shootings and hangings and things that happened in the recent past. Remember, it was still the Indian Nations right up to 1907 when that part of the country became the eastern half of the new state of Oklahoma.

Anyway, these stories appalled my mother and delighted me and she did everything she could to keep such things from my delicate ears.

I couldn't tell her I was storing up material for stories to be written. I didn't know it myself. But how grateful I was thirty years later to have those stories I heard confirmed by the record of Parker's court kept in the Fort Worth branch of the National Archives, and the newspapers published in Fort Smith at the time, and then Glenn Shirley's book, *Law West of Fort Smith.*

Those Ft. Smith stories were close to the source of most of my other tales, the Winslow hills. Because Pearl Starr, Ft. Smith tenderloin madam and daughter of the infamous Belle, bought a house on West Mountain at Winslow where she had a care-taker couple keep her little daughter. Away from all that Ft. Smith sin.

Pearl Starr could visit her little girl during periods of slow business in the lust trade I suppose, just by boarding the Frisco at Ft. Smith and in little over an hour be in Winslow and take one of the resort hotel horse cabs up West Mountain. There were a lot of resort hotels in Winslow then, and plenty of public transportation.

That child caused green-eyed envy among local children because she rode to school each day on a fine little Shetland pony.

Grandfather wasn't the rural letter carrier yet. He was partner in a general mercantile store called Stockburger & Miller where they had a fancy inventory including Persian rugs. It was a grocery, too, and Grandfather delivered foodstuff to the Starr place, which was a big house set well back from the road behind wire fences. He was about the only local who got inside that fence.

> There were always men around the Starr place, he said. They were all strangers. Oklahoma men, I expect. They weren't very friendly. They never spoke

> to me. Friends of Pearl Starr, or maybe her mother. I never tried to nose into their affairs or what they were doing up there. They looked like the kind of men who didn't take kindly to anybody who wanted to make conversation.

Then one day a lot of those Persian rugs were missing and probably without warrant the town constable went into the Starr house and found the carpets. So the next time Pearl Starr came to visit her little girl, she was arrested and taken to Fayetteville to stand trial.

Nothing came of it.

> I expect some of old Belle's fancy lawyers came up from Ft. Smith and the rugs were returned and there were a lot of apologies about misunderstanding.

Only one thing dangerous ever happened to Grandfather at the Starr place. In a deep hole near the house where a tree had been dug up, there was a white-tail deer fawn trapped there and Grandfather jumped down into the hole to help the little Bambi out.

> Well, I got it out but he fought me and those little hooves were like razors and I went back to town bleeding like a fresh liver.

Those weren't wild, tall tales. They were all, each and every one, based solidly on fact. So all a good novelist had to do was create a few of his own people, give them a story, and plop them right down in the middle of that real stuff. Bang! Historical novel.

And everything wasn't furious and savage, either. Some of the best memories were how compassion by their neighbors saved a lot of people from starvation during the Great Depression. Each fall when he slaughtered hogs,

Grandfather carried pork loin and cracklins to the families on his mail route who needed it most, the ones who didn't have the money to get to California.

They repaid him, even in the years long after the Depression, by having him speak the funeral service over the graves of their fathers and mothers. And over themselves.

In that time, Grandmother placed Franklin Roosevelt in an exalted seat. For her, there was a hierarchy that led from God through Jesus to F.D.R. and then Dizzy Dean, the pitcher for the Saint Louis Cardinals. Don't ask me how Dizzy Dean got in there.

No one ever asked her. After all, with a big woman who could kill rattlesnakes by throwing rocks at them from twenty feet, who could handle a team of mules as well as any man, who could use a two-bitted axe like it was a hatchet, who could feed thirty people cooking on a cast-iron wood stove and all hot and delicious when it came to the table, you didn't ask questions.

You knew she had no more than a fourth grade education. You knew about the time she was cornered in the barn by a big milk cow with a nasty disposition and she got out by hitting the cow between the eyes with her fist. Breaking most of the bones in her hand. But the cow backed off and never tried to bully her again.

Franklin Roosevelt's people built Grandmother a new privy with a concrete base. The WPA or the PWA or some such thing. She called it her "Roosevelt" and used it each day, whether she needed to or not.

And there was the CCC. A regular army officer and a few non-commissioned officers and a cook went out there in the boondocks at Devil's Den with a bunch of guys and started building stuff. And at White Rock Mountain, too. Roads and bridges and picnic tables and cabins. All still there today.

And the men came in from Devil's Den on Saturday night, carried in army trucks, and sat in the Winslow Machine Shop where beer was served, and they sang and danced together and sometimes spilled out into the streets for an old fashioned fist fight and all the citizens sat on their front porches in the dark, sipping iced tea and remarking that it was almost as entertaining as when the Holy-Rollers came and put up a tent on the high school playground and fished for souls.

And baseball was the heart of the summer, just as basketball was the same for winter. Even a small high school, that had no chance of fielding a football team, could collect half a dozen kids to run up and down a clay court gym floor in their underwear, bouncing a round ball.

And it went on from Winslow to the County Seat for history. Like Mr. Brown, who had one of these neighborhood grocery stores across the street from my grammar school. And one day Bonnie Parker and Clyde Barrow drove up and Clyde asked for cigarettes and Mr. Brown, recognizing the infamous pair of killers from newpaper photos, dumped an armload of smokes onto the counter and Clyde Barrow laughed and said he only wanted a single deck and threw down a quarter and left.

Oh yeah! I lived in that neighborhood and did I ever make plenty of the situation. Some wide-eyed kid would come from the south side and I'd stand there in front of Brown's.

> "Right there," I'd say. "Bonnie and Clyde just a few days before they was shot dead down in Texas. Or Oklahoma. And right over there they parked their car and just sat there, cleaned a couple of Browning Automatic Rifles."
>
> "Geeez!"
>
> "All the local police, heard Bonnie and Clyde was comin, went fishin'! Outa town, man!"

> "Geeez!"
>
> "I lived in Ft. Smith then, and when they killed Bonnie and Clyde, daddy took me to see the car they'd been shot in. A navy blue B model Ford. Shot all to hell, man! They had it in a Ford agency close to Texas Corner in Ft. Smith and it cost a dime apiece to see it! Shot all to hell, man!"
>
> "Geeez! Hey did you see it like that when they killed Pretty Boy Floyd?"
>
> "Are you crazy! They didn't kill Pretty Boy Floyd in no car! They just shot him in a field in Georgia or someplace then brought him back to Salisaw to bury him. My Uncle Legette went to the funeral."

Can anybody who hears and feels that kind of stuff avoid putting it down on a piece of paper? I hope not. Can anybody who experiences that pulse of life in a certain time and a specific place rest easy with the prospect of dying without giving the new generations a taste of what it is like? I couldn't.

Here in the hills, we're so close to what we were. Most of us don't even know that, but for the few who do, isn't there an obligation to pass it on?

In about 1985, some of us were driving to White Rock, through the wild, rugged hills and timber. And we stopped at one point and walked around in the woods and I found a bench mark. Barely concealed under a blanket of dead oak leaves.

A bench mark is a place on the ground where surveyors show the result of their work. It's displayed on a topographical map by little triangles. On the ground, it's a concrete post buried so only the top shows and on the top is a brass plaque.

The brass plaque on the bench mark I stumbled onto in that wild White Rock wilderness indicated the elevation above sea level, the longitude and latitude and the date of the survey. The date was 1935. It made the hair stand up on my neck. It still does. Because it meant that the interior of the Ozarks, only a short walk, really, from towns and railroads and highways and cheeseburgers, had been virgin of manmade grids from the time it had been molten magma until one hundred thirty-five years *after* Tom Jefferson bought it, sight unseen, from Napoleon.

Sure, you read and you watch and you listen and you remember. But if you really want to write, there's got to be that secret charge of electric passion up the backbone at the mention of fox hounds running or any other thing that sets the senses to churning.

In a recent study, Barry Sanders, Professor of English at Pitzer College in California wrote that the old wise men of the Maya Indians who told the stories of their people down the generations were called Echo Man. Because to be effective, they had to listen and relay back to the people important lessons of their on-going tribal story.

Maybe all these authors who praise the Ozarks are Echo Man. Not that they had the opportunity to hear the verbal tales of the early settlers. But maybe some of the music is a song of the land itself.

There is no poet and very few good novelists or historians who don't admit that certain environments speak to them.

So maybe writers of Northwest Arkansas hear the voice of the rocks and trees, the mountains and streams. Which surely must include the ghosts of long since departed Old Breed word merchants who created the oral tradition, the myth and legend and history of this sacred place. Lying there like the sandstone grave markers in forgotten burial grounds. Moss covered, ancient, wordless.

But waiting to be written down.

Jory Sherman

Jory Sherman has published more than 150 books since 1965. He has published over 500 short stories and 1000 articles since beginning his writing career. His poetry had appeared in a number of literary journals.

Sherman's love for the outdoors is reflected in two collections of Ozark pieces and short stories, *My Heart is in the Ozarks*, published by The First Ozark Press and *An Early Frost*, published by White Oak Press.

The Medicine Horn, published in hardcover in 1992, won the prestigious Spur award presented by Western Writers of America in the category, Best Novel of the West.

His novel, *Grass Kingdom*, published in 1994 by Tor under its new Forge imprint, was nominated for a Pulitzer Prize in Letters.

Sherman currently lives near Forsyth, Missouri.

Painting the Scene

We who live and write in the Ozarks are particularly lucky when it comes to writing descriptions of landscapes or describing scenes of beauty and wonder. And, we have such a diversity of peoples from all over the world, that we have little trouble in fleshing out characters in our stories and novels. For, if we can see, we can draw and paint pictures with words. If we can accomplish this, we can add vividness and reality to our scenes.

While the following pertains to the novel, particularly, in general any scene in fiction or non-fiction, long or short, can benefit from the principles under examination.

There is the form. There is the content. In constructing a novel, these are not separate elements, but Janus-faces of the same paradigm. I view the novel as a series of scenes, all linked together by the double-helix fiber of form and content. Because scenes are the building blocks of the novel, they deserve care in visualization and construction.

I am a visual thinker, so when constructing a scene my tendency is to think like a painter. If you are to paint with words, you might view the blank page much as an artist will approach an empty canvas. Basically, we are using caricature when writing a scene, exaggerating certain elements, viewing some characters in close-up, keeping others in the background. In some scenes we need the long, panoramic view, but still must thread the prose-painting, the scene, with color, design, pattern and action.

The writer must deal with action, with noise or silence, with weather, with seasons, with personality and the human mind. The scenes are first seen as mental images, sometimes stark or static until viewed in detail. Then, it becomes a matter of mixing elements, moving people behind a proscenium arch, across a stage, if you will, daubing in smaller details that add depth and weight to the whole. This is so that the reader's attention is drawn to a particular element important to the story, or to the characters. The writer's ability to control a scene insures that the reader will not lose interest. It is the author's task to create a scene that is vibrant with action, with movement, with the very breath of life itself. Of course, this is only an illusion, the magic that makes a reader *believe* that the scene is real.

When drawing a scene, an image comes to my mind and I begin to prepare for it just as the artist prepares the empty canvas for the painting. I may sketch in the blue of the sky over a coating of liquid white and then build my clouds, sketch in skyline and put distant mountains along the horizon. Then, it's time to draw the brush down with the sky colors and paint in grass, a cabin, horses, trees, shadows. When looking at nature, I look for light and shadow and my eye frames the vision, shuts out the elements to be eliminated if one painted from life.

One need not use any words denoting actual colors when describing a scene. The human mind makes powerful connections when the language suggests a tone or a color. In a semantical sense, we associate certain objects, animals, seasons, times of day with colors. As an example, here is a scene from an essay I wrote called "The Painting of Landscapes in Winter," which appeared in my book *My Heart Is In the Ozarks*.

> There is sun here but it's gauzy like a kerosene lamp in a hurricane. It splashes light on the bare ground, fries a dead oak leaf with a mild current, and lingers on the north side of trees like a yellow mold. Down the slope on the arm of Lake Taneycomo, the mushy light gets tangled in the still waters like melted strands of a spider web turning to butter. A doe, heavy with unborn fawn, creeps along the ridge, its nostrils rubbery, blowing steamy smoke into the tawny air of morning.

In the above passage there are images which produce the effect of colors in the mind. Words like "gauzy" evoke an airy whiteness, and even "kerosene lamp" produces an image of orange light against a black background ("hurricane"). "Bare ground"' is also laden with a particular color and when followed by the phrase, "fries a dead oak leaf with a mild current," we can "see" colors. Even "rubbery nostrils," tells us not only the way a doe's nostrils move, but that they are black, like rubber. Steamy smoke contrasts with the "tawny air" of morning.

In the following scene there is a sparse use of color. Dark shades, with splashes of pale yellow or ocher, are used in the opening to set a tone of grimness. After this somber mood is established, the bright colors bleed a startling splotch on the scene in sharp contrast to the black canvas.

This is the opening scene of my novel, *Winter of the Wolf*, published in hardcover by Walker & Co., and in paperback by Tor Books. I have highlighted the colors used in the scene.

> The man on the Indian pony, a **steeldust gray**, picked his way over the rimrock, his eyes restless beads in moveable sockets, the flesh at the corners squinched to block the blinding glint of weak sun on snow. The big Hawken .54, the **brass** patchbox **dulled** and **mottled** by weather and time, rested easy in his right hand, the barrel laid across the shoulder of the plain cowhide pommel, the stock balanced on the calf of his elkskin-clad leg. He was big, even in his oversized sheepskin-lined antelope coat, the sleeves and bottom fringed to draw rain from its surface. He wore a **dark** felt hat cut from a thick bolt, and five days of **coal black** beard. His features were flattened under high cheekbones that were divided in a symmetrical design by a nose that had been broken at least once at the bridge, giving it the angular shape of a hawk's beak.
>
> Draped across the gray's rump, behind the flared cantle of his Denver saddle, a pair of fresh lion skins flapped with each rocking movement of the horse. A **dark** broom of hair, still **green** and uncured, torn from an Arapaho's scalp, hung from the saddlehorn by a tough strand of sinew. Two other scalplocks, long, silky, and rust **red**, tied at the stumps with water-blotched **pink** ribbons, dangled from the horn on the opposite side of the pommel.

To the discerning reader, there are other colors in the scene that pepper the description. These words are **rust, sheepskin-lined**, **antelope**, and **elkskin-lined**. The mind fills in the colors from these images. Even the phrase **weak sun** gives off a pale yellow color that imparts a sense of bleakness to the mountain painting.

In creating a scene, the magic occurs when all the elements come together into a cohesive, resonant, symmetrical design. Light and shadow form a picture, a background at first, where we can carve our buildings and figures, place objects in relationships. Because writing is fluid, we can then zoom down to the scene and go for close-ups. We can enter a cabin shown in longshot and paint another scene. We can put furniture where we want it, place a figure in a chair or on a bed, show a man or a woman shoving sticks of kindling in a firebox.

By visualizing every step of construction, the novelist can paint vivid images in the reader's mind, can harmonize colors that appeal to the senses, can place elements within the scene that add to its verisimilitude. Sometimes, these elements can and should be minute details that do not bear heavily on the story or on character, but help the reader to see, to feel, to hear, what the writer intends. As in a painting, the writer is attempting to achieve balance and form while transmitting a vitality to the page that makes the reader plunge into the writer's world and live in it for the duration of the book.

Here is a single paragraph from "Something of September," which also appeared in *My Heart Is In The Ozarks*.

> The soft colors of the sky, smeared like an empty bed of faded blues and reds. The framing trees on the bluff, thrust there against the sky like cuneiform messages in urgent green swords.

This suggests the pageantry of colors in the sky at sunset. In another piece from the same book entitled "Evening at Summerend," I describe an evening scene in the opening paragraph.

> Gold touches the porches. Gold threads through the evening fields, limns the grass, the white-brown backs of cattle grazing. Sunset coming on, glazing the pond with a miracle of alchemy: more gold, more of the sun's straight rays as it sinks here and rises somewhere in the far Pacific Ocean. Rises in blood over blue waters, green islands.

In "Mid-Summer In the Ozarks," I attempt to describe what the light is like at a particular time of year.

> Some of the summer settles on my orange shoulder.
>
> On children. Flaring up like sudden flowers in a fallow field. Flaming over the landscape, full of July, fat with the summer center of the year. Orange and burnt umber and freckled brown.

In the previous paragraph, even the use of the word "fallow" allows me to paint the field yellow without mentioning the word "yellow," for the use of the word "flowers" so close to "fallow" conjures up the image. This is what is so remarkable about the English language. Word associations can prove very powerful when juxtaposing images. Even the word "flaring" in the same sentence, contributes to the overall image of color. We sometimes paint with words, with language.

In the following scene, the opening to my novel, *Horne's Law*, also published by Walker and Tor in hard/soft, paints a scene of icy chill with its bleak, frosty colors. In my mind, the scene began with a phrase that I decided not to use: **In the blue air of morning. . .** I saw this blue-tinted tableau where a lone man walked his trapline in winter and so reworked the scene to impart a sense of isolation and danger.

> He strode through the **blue** shadows of that winter morn, a tall rawboned man whose step was careful on the narrow, winding trail just above the creek. The cold, **slate-colored** water burbled, whispering soft against the **snow-flocked** banks. The creek made its own song in the odd stillness of morning as the **pale** mountain jay, ghostly against the **gray** shroud of **snowscape**, marked Horne's progress along

> the trapline. The jay flitted from spruce to fir to pine, stirring the silence with its clawed scratch on the icy scales of trembling branches. Clumps of **snow** fell from each thin, sinewy limb where the bird perched, plopped with muffled thuds on the **snow-covered** earth.

The word **snow** is used as a color throughout, a repetitive thread that emphasizes the ponderous whiteness of the scene.

We might view the scene as a film director or cinematographer will perceive the Master Shot. I tend to create scenes in this manner, first visualizing the entire scene, then adding or subtracting elements as I write. It would be boring to write in every tiny detail of a room or a location, but it is not boring to weave a spell by using the technique of caricature, portraying some elements in extreme close-up, others in varying degrees of size in the background.

By using colors and tones, we can create the mood we need to emphasize the action in the scene. The English language is rich with colors we can use. It's a giant Crayola box of colors and the novelist has the freedom to use them all, to blend them, to play light on them and bring light out of them.

Since English is the richest language in the world, we have so many ways to build a perfect scene, to create a mood, to bring tensile strength and tension to the action, the images. Our language is rich in vowels and consonants, short words and long words, borrowed words and coined words–clay and wire, chromatic scales on which to create thunders and whispers, fanfares and dirges, all sorts of sounds and images that bring writing to life. We can fashion sentences that vibrate with the staccato force of an air drill, or flow mellifluously through the air like burbling spring water over round stones. We can achieve tonal clarity and rich harmony just by painting our scenes with well-chosen words juxtapositioned like colors on a palette roiling together under the swirl and tap of a fine camel hair brush. We can stroke and shape the language to depict a scene that penetrates the reader's mind, makes him or her part of the story, an involved participant in the magic of language.

The word "chromatic" is both musical and a linguistic term. The word denotes both color and a scale of musical notes. But, then, the artist draws from the poet, the poet from the painter, the sculptor and so, too do the great composers draw inspiration from the playwrights, the poets, the painters, the sculptors, the novelists.

And all art, like all things, is superbly connected and there should be, in the writer's vocabulary, all the colors of the spectrum on his palette, the contours and graceful lines wrought by the sculptor's chisel and chromatic language of the musical composer so that all the disparate elements of a scene in literature becomes a cohesive whole, a painting that sings and occupies space in the universe–and one might then come upon a most beautiful stone structure that sings in the reader's imagination like a mellifluous figure played on a harp, rhythmic and chromatic, visually appealing to the eye and mind.

If the writer pays close attention to drawing the scene, this will help him or her, also, since the first scene must be linked to the second, the second to the third, and so on. We don't write whole books all at once. Instead, we write small, interconnected scenes. We may hold a giant canvas in our minds, but we must paint in small patches, blend everything together so that we achieve a unified whole that would be incomplete if any single scene were removed. In this sense, the novelist is a film cutter, working with single images that when run at twenty-four frames a second give the impression of continuous flow and graceful, natural movement. We do time shifts and transitions from scene to scene, cutting from one shot to the next, but retaining continuity. This, too, is an art, for the scene by itself is merely a fragment, a small portion of the entire painting. The positioning of scenes in relation to one another is what gives the novel its life, its movement, its solidity and symmetry, its structure, its sense, its form, its content. All of the scenes, taken in the writer's order, comprise the novel as the author intends it. If the novel is well conceived and constructed, then the reader will not think of each little scene as separate parts, but see the whole book as the author originally visualized it, as a story of people during a special time of their lives.

Writing is magic.

Yet, beneath the trickery, there is technique and instinct, pattern, design.

Beginning writers often ask me how to write a novel. I ask them what their idea of writing a novel might be. They almost always think of the book as being an insurmountable obstacle, something unattainable, a huge mountain to climb. That is because they are thinking of length and size, instead of a collection of integrated scenes.

I always think of a novel in terms of size, too. In the beginning, when the concept first begins to take shadowy, embryonic shape, I picture the novel as a completed work. I see the cover, the title, the byline, the illustration, the blurb. But, after I've plotted the novel and written a summary, I see the work only in terms of scenes. Not in terms of chapters. There can be several scenes within a chapter, or simply a single scene that serves its purpose.

Writing the scene is the key to writing the novel, whether it be 50,000 words or 500,000 words.

I believe that great care must be taken in writing these small fragments that make up the mosaic of a novel.

In each scene, I ask myself many questions. What do I want to show? Do I want the reader to feel the bone-numbing chill of winter? Do I want to portray the slashing razors of a blue norther, or the earth-cracking heat of a blazing 120 degree sun in Arizona? Do I want to strobe light a specific, important character, or keep a significant personage in low light at the back of the room? There are always a number of choices to be made when drawing a scene and the reward comes when you hit the target on one of them, when the chroma is blindingly intense and bright on the canvas.

The subtle use of color in a scene can add depth and resonance to the action.

Here is a description of Lemuel Hawke in *The Medicine Horn*, published in hardcover by Tor Books, as he stalks two Indians in the woods. This is Lem's first sighting of an Indian and he knows the Indian has killed at least one white man. He is only sixteen years old at the time.

> Lem felt his blood surge out of his brain fast as water down a rainspout. He felt lightheaded, giddy as a kid sipping fermented cider. His temples drummed with a rapid thunder.
>
> His heart turned wild as a flushed timberdoodle, seemed as if it would jump from his ribcage. The Indian, standing next to a scaly bark hickory, was so **gaudy** with feathers and **orange** roach, Lem had the almost uncontrollable urge to rub the **bright pigments** from his eyes.
>
> The tip of his nose began to itch from an unseen irritation. A gnat discovered the **glassy** water of his eye, flew at it like a miller against a **lighted** windowpane.
>
> The Indian seemed part of the tree, part of the forest. Lem stretched his neck and more of the savage came into view. Still, he could see only the bare **bronze** of the Indian's back, the **bright** plumage dangling like a gutted ringneck pheasant from his still roach, the long rifle in his hand studded with **brass** tacks along its

> stock, a single goose feather twirling on a thong attached to the frontplate. The Indian wore a breechclout over his deerskin leggings, a knife in a **beaded** leather sheath. An iron tomahawk jutted from a wide, **colorful** cloth sash that girded his midsection.

A few moments later, Lem sees the other Indian.

> . . .forty-some yards beyond, crouched behind a grassy mound, ferns and saplings sprouting profusely in **emerald** fountains over its surface.

The Indians stand in contrast to their surroundings. Against the green and brown of the woods, they are startling to behold, with their orange roaches and beads, iron tomahawks and brass-studded rifles. Later in closeup, we see the Indians' painted faces, hideous and frightening to a young man facing death all alone.

The scene, ultimately, consists of a small area that can stay tight or enlarge and project, foreshadow other events to come, refer to previous events or just create a single, dynamic moment in time.

I wanted to show a moment of epiphany in the following scene, from *Eagles of Destiny*, published by Zebra, to portray Estrellita in transition from a young girl to a woman in love. She is dining with her parents, her chaperone, a soldier, Merito, and the man to whom she is betrothed in St. Louis' Planter's House in 1833. Although the marriage pact was made when she and Augustino were children, she has met the American, Jeremiah York and fallen in love with him. She has just defended him to those at the table, angering Augustino.

Without a word being spoken, each person present sees Estrellita, not as a child, but as a full-blown woman. And, it's all done with light and shadow, intense flashes of brilliant color.

Estrellita caught the **dark**, lancing look and tossed her head defiantly, fixing him (Augustino) with a haughty gaze. The afternoon **sunlight** streamed through the nearby window, washed her **olive** complexion with a **golden** spray, bathed her face until it shone with a startling, beauteous **glow**.

Augustino stifled a gasp as he looked at her face, saw the lovely contours illuminated, carved by **light** to perfection. The sun seemed trapped in the sleek, **dark** depths of her tresses, boiling molten **gold** and hammered foil into each silken strand. Her cheekbones stood out in finely chiseled relief and her eyes flashed with sparks like the flickering **lights** in **diamonds** or **sapphires**. Her lips pouted with a moist invitation. He wanted to touch her, crush her lips against his. For a long moment he stared at her and did not realize his fingers were trembling as if expressing the desire that flared in his veins like ignited **phosphor**, gnawed like soft fur **afire**, at his loins.

Merito, as well, was struck with this sudden **illumination** of her rare beauty. He glanced sideways at Augustino and then at her father, Don Miguel. Both men seemed frozen in the awesome **radiance** of her beauty, just as he, too, was held transfixed for a moment as though turned to stone.

Don Miguel looked at his daughter and memories flooded to his brain in a flutter of images. He saw the chubbiness of her baby face swept away by the **light**, remembered her sweet child's smile, and realized that Estrellita was a woman grown and become more beautiful than he could ever have imagined. He saw the child in her too, and he saw the woman, saw the grace and bearing of her mother, and her mother's forebears, the strong bloodlines in the **sunstruck** profile of her face, the savage heritage of an Indian ancestor visible as a raw smear of **vermillion** across her cheek.

And the men at the table fell in love with Estrellita in that special moment when the sun poured

> over her like **honey** and **highlighted** her loveliness. They fell in love with her in different ways and for all time because they knew she was no ordinary woman, but a Thoroughbred, a champion sleek and fleet and strong-minded, who would demand a very strong man to tame her wild heart, to temper the savage **blood** that flowed in her veins as the **lava** flows from a restless volcano.
>
> Her mother saw the looks in the men's eyes and so, too, did Lucia, whose face **darkened** like a stormcloud and whose pulse raced with long-forgotten tremors.
>
> "Yes," choked her mother, "we must be leaving. Let us return to the hacienda to complete our preparations for the fiesta."
>
> But no one moved, for the sun still **glistened** on Estrellita's face and rippled in her hair, gently brushed faint **shadows** across her lips like an invisible kiss, like a kiss from a forbidden and secret lover.

Even words like **blood** and **lava** bring color to the scene very subtly and need not be emphasized with chromatic adjectives. Words like **radiance**, **glistened**, and **brilliance** further add to the highlighting of Estrellita as the centerpiece of this scene.

Always, there is the magic and the mystery of writing in making a scene come alive. But, as novelists, that is our goal. We want readers to experience the magic without seeing the hands move. We want them to bring their eyes and heart to the experience of the novel without seeing the artist at work.

Show the reader what you want the reader to see. Paint the scene with colors to make it vibrant. Make the reader feel what you feel. Use the chromatic scales of the language. Make magic.

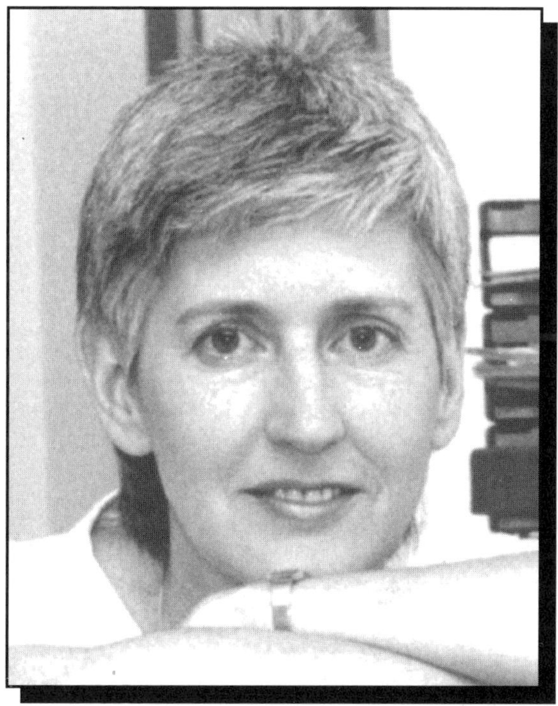

Joan Brix Banks

Joan Banks began freelancing in 1978 and has been published in a wide range of periodicals ranging from *American Baby* to *Ranger Rick's*.

A book contract with Berkley Publishing Group inspired her to resign her position as director of the Joplin, Missouri, Public Library in 1988 to write full time. Her fourth suspense novel, *Blood Ties*, appears under the pseudonym Alexa Brix. One of her earlier novels, *Gently Down the Stream*, has been published in Norway.

A native of Tulsa, Oklahoma, Banks currently lives in Joplin with her husband, a son, a cat, two dogs, three guineas, four ducks, and six geese. Her daughter is married and lives in New Jersey.

What If and Maybe

I began to wonder what had happened to my husband as I watched pages of local ads flop over a clock gizmo in an El Dorado Springs, Missouri, cafe. He'd excused himself to go to the restroom, while I was polishing off a piece of allegedly homemade apple pie. I'd finished that task, but still he hadn't returned.

How long do I wait before I go back and knock on the restroom door? I asked myself.

People came and went, letting bursts of the sweltering August heat in the front door. Still I waited. I made a motion to get up when my peripheral vision caught someone coming my way, but it was just the waitress, asking once again if she could get me something. Minutes ticked by.

Finally, he did come back, but as we were driving away I asked him: "What if you hadn't returned?"

That *what if* was the genesis of my second novel, *Edge of Darkness*.

Where do you get your ideas is the most frequent question I'm asked. Most of them spring from such ordinary incidents as the one above.

In the book, a man and his wife are traveling in the Ozarks, and they stop at a small town cafe. As they go in, the husband notices a sign in the window, "Waitress wanted." He jests with his wife about how she could probably get a job there. They have lunch, then he goes to the restroom. She waits. Of course, in the book, the husband doesn't come back; he has disappeared without a trace.

Finally, the wife has to do something. First she searches, enlisting the aide of the proprietor, then they call the sheriff. He has no more clue than she does about what has happened, so he advises her to go home, saying he'll file a missing persons report and keep in touch. After several days at home, the woman is going crazy with the waiting. So she abandons her contact lenses for her old glasses and she cuts, bleaches, and perms her hair. Remember the sign in the window? Waitress wanted? She does. She goes back to the town, applies for the job and gets it, and starts to investigate her husband's disappearance.

> [She] rehearsed her new role all the way to Westmost, not apprehensively, but oddly excited about the whole thing. Assuming a new life was perhaps a fantasy many people nurtured but seldom had the impetus to try. Now she had compelling reasons to do so, not the least of which was to break out of the waiting that had all but incapacitated her. She was *doing something.*
>
> *Edge of Darkness*, Charter, 1989

When people used to ask me why I didn't write a novel (before I was writing fiction), I usually retorted with "I don't have anything to say." As I read more and more novels, I realized a lot of those writers didn't have much to say either. I liked reading certain authors, and I found a growing desire to create the ambience for others that those writers created for me. As I began writing fiction, I discovered I did have some things I wanted to say. One idea that had been perking in my head was that some poor person could be out hiking and stumble upon someone's marijuana operation. In one innocent moment, he or she could get blown away. I wanted to say something about that. So I created a situation where I could explore that – not in a pedantic way, but just in the course of a story. The idea simmered in my brain for several years before I found a story line.

Experiences a writer creates for him or herself are germs that grow into novels. During a visit to the International Wolf Center in Ely, Minnesota, I read about a learning vacation being offered by Vermilion Community College there. I signed up and spent a week learning *how* to track and tracking radio-collared wolves. Eight of us, all strangers, were housed in a tiny cabin on a Minnesota Lake. We joked that the study was probably about us, not wolves – seeing how strangers would cope with crowded conditions and sleep deprivation (we each spent two all-night shifts in a radio-equipped van). The experience made me want to set a book in northern Minnesota, but I didn't have a plot in mind.

Shortly after I returned home, I was browsing in a used bookstore when the title, *Survival Poaching*, practically leaped off the shelf at me. The book was an education in the ways of securing illegal game. By this time, I was reading every outdoor magazine I could get my hands on – looking for something that would hook my interest. And I found it in several articles about the U.S. Wildlife Service's war on the poaching of black bears for their gall bladders, which are considered an aphrodisiac in the Orient, and their paws and teeth, which are sold for souvenirs. I had the background I wanted.

> She hunkered forward and chanced another look from behind her cover. The three men were still struggling with the mother bear; two of the others had the cub's lifeless body and were dragging it nearer. . .

> Sandy was glad their bodies masked her view of what was happening. Her imagination made it graphic enough. . .
>
> Blood Ties (by Alexa Brix, pseudonym), Diamond, 1992

Because I'm not from northern Minnesota, I created a heroine who wasn't either. She could be as naive as I am about the area, seeing it from a fresh viewpoint. I mention that because of the old writer's adage: write what you know. It's only partially true. We can learn about things. Certainly I didn't know about bear poaching. But we have to be on our toes when we step outside our normal milieu. Jon Cleary, the Australian author of the book, *The Sundowners*, brought this home to me. He wrote a book called *Twister* that was set in a fictional town in southwest Missouri. I've been told that he made a hurried trip to Neosho to do research. Maybe to people in Australia and even in other states, the setting seems authentic, but the moment Cleary referred to the road as *macadam* he lost me. Around here we call it blacktop, as in "Go two miles down here to the blacktop. . ." By having my character be out of her element, she didn't have to be as authentic to the region as if she had been a native.

Once I had the poaching background in mind, I began developing the characters, one of whom was an undercover person with U.S. Fish and Wildlife, whose name I won't mention here for reasons that will soon be apparent. I wrote the book and, feeling as if I were sending my child off into the world, put the manuscript in the mail. To celebrate, I went on vacation.

You know how it is when you return: grass needs mowing, mail needs sorting. I started shoving the pounds of bulk mail and magazines aside, concentrating on the first class stuff. But one *Newsweek* begged to be picked up for no obvious reason. I thumbed through it, and an article on poaching caught my eye. I did a double take. The article spotlighted a fish and wildlife undercover agent with the same name as my character. Undoubtedly in all my reading, I'd come across his name and deposited it in my subconscious. When I was naming my characters, his name popped up and felt absolutely right, as well it should have.

I gulped, marveling at the serendipity that had caused me to open that particular magazine, and picked up the phone. My editor was able to make the switch before the galleys were printed. Of course, there will always be real people with the names of your characters, but this one had too many characteristics similar to the real McCoy, a man of sterling qualities. Perhaps the real life agent wouldn't have minded; my character, after all, was one of the good guys.

My characters aren't people I know; most of them are probably me. Yes, even the bad guys. I confess I have murderous thoughts at times; what sets me apart from the villains in my books is that I have impulse control.

It seems to me there are lots of villains in the world. Some of them make up the hate groups we hear about in the news. The paranoia of these people seems to create the world they so decry. This was another one of those ideas floating around in my head, and I was ripe for a way to explore it, but couldn't seem to find it.

Then one day a friend and I decided to go canoeing. I assumed she knew a back paddle from a brace; she assumed I was the expert. Neither of us knew a bird about it. As we struggled to get the canoe off the car, I noticed that we'd caught the attention of a fisherman nearby. Finally, we launched our canoe and climbed in. The current caught it, and before we knew it, we were across the creek and floundering, on a rocky spit. Was the fisherman stifling a laugh?

My friend had the presence of mind to loudly announce, "Well, here we are."

Two women canoeing in the wilderness struck me as an idea full of possibilities for jeopardy. Then I remembered the tragedy of the highway patrolman who was killed south of Springfield, Missouri, by a member of a white supremacist group. What if, I thought, I create a simultaneous story of a neo-Nazi cop-killer running from the police? What if we know his path will cross that of my heroine?

That's the scenario for my third novel, *Gently Down the Stream*. The river in the book is wilder than the Buffalo National River, but the bluffs I wrote about are those at the Ozark campground on the Buffalo. Artistic license let me put those bluffs on both sides of a narrowly-channeled river.

> Stains left from organic material formed veils of black along the vertical surfaces, almost like paintings by some modern artist. Any other time she would have wished for her camera, but now she was concentrating on how to get out of this natural prison. . . Unfortunately nature made no inviting path. Cracks in the rock would have to do for hand- and footholds. Her hand groped for a fissure and found one, and inch by inch she worked her way upward.
>
> *Gently Down the Stream*, Berkley, 1991

It takes my character, Susan Morrow, several pages to get up that bluff, and of course, more terror awaits at the top. I envisioned her climb while floating in an inner tube, gazing upward at the peaceful sky. The birds, the sounds, the smells fed my imagination. The town of Breedlove was patterned on the way I remembered Jasper, Arkansas, although when I go back there, the similarities are minor: mainly the courthouse on the square. Still, I feel a certain kinship with the town. I see something and secretly think – there's the store Jan went in. Weird, huh? But you do really begin to believe in these characters you create.

The canoe trip was the catalyst. It furnished the

vehicle for me to explore hate groups on paper. My research into hate groups began in earnest: I read everything I could find. I was shocked at the plans and schemes these people had in mind for their fellow Americans, shocked to learn about the people who had been murdered, the crimes that had been committed. The editor decided my first scenario, based on a plot that had been uncovered, was too evil, so instead I had the character plant a bomb in a federal building. Would anyone believe this? I wondered. Would anyone believe such acts of terrorism could happen in the United States? This was before The World Trade Center bombing, before Oklahoma City. In the book, though, one man, a senator, had an ounce of goodness, and he revealed the plan in time to have the building evacuated. Oklahoma City showed us that reality can be harsher than fiction.

That *what if* that spawned my first book came about when I was talking to my friend who was an insurance claims representative. By wide area telephone line, she handled calls in a state far distant from where she lived. So, I asked, what if she overheard a murder?

> Lora, scarcely breathing, quickly disconnected. She was holding the emery board poised for another stroke.
>
> What could she do? The woman was in obvious trouble, but was it just a domestic problem? She didn't know the woman's name or where she was calling from, except somewhere in the state of New York.
>
> Lora rubbed the frown that had formed between her eyebrows and pulled the headset off. There didn't seem to be anything to do.
>
> *Death Claim*, Charter, 1988

What if the murderer realized the crime had an auditory witness? What if he knew who she was and where she was? What if, what if. . . ? The wheels started turning; details had to be thought out. *Maybes* had to be explored. Maybe the heroine didn't know he knew. Maybe he flew to where she lived. And the plot thickened.

When someone approaches me with a one-line "idea that will make a great novel," I want to roll my eyes. A single idea isn't a great novel. A novel is a tapestry of woof and warp that takes a long time to weave. Sitting in a chair long enough to do so is one of the toughest things about writing. I make a lot of trips to stare into the refrigerator.

In the midst of plotting, I become consumed by it, certain that I can never pull it off. When I get that look in my eye and start bandying about my *what ifs*, my family groans. My husband hardly wants to get in the car with me because he knows he'll be trapped. Sometimes getting a plot out of your brain almost hurts. It resists. But the *what ifs* and *maybes* finally succeed.

What if she did. . .
What if he went. . .
Maybe she could call. . .
Maybe he can tell. . .

What ifs and *maybes* are tools a writer can use to give ideas shape, turning them into the absorbing escapism we call fiction.

Photo: Jory Sherman

Charlotte Sherman

Charlotte Sherman has published thirty-one books in the last fifteen years. Influenced by her husband, writer Jory Sherman, she began writing westerns in 1980. After twenty-nine westerns, she had her first romance, *A Kiss at Sunrise*, published in 1993.

Her short story, "A Rose for Christmas", published in Zebra's 1994 Christmas anthology, *The Joy of Christmas*, won an award from the Missouri Writers Guild in 1995.

Sherman's latest novel, *Country Lovesong*, is set in the Branson music scene and was released in June 1995.

She resides in Forsyth, Missouri where she is active in several writers' organizations and is currently working on a woman of the west novel.

Romancing the Ozarks

Living in the Ozarks is a romance.

Among these gentle hills and hollows, on these lakes and streams, romance flourishes, for the beauty here touches the heart, fills it with all the emotions of love, sets the blood to tingling in every vein.

It seems that everyone likes a touching love story, whether it's incorporated into a book, a poem, a movie or a song. Love is immortalized in Robert Browning's poem "Let Me Count the Ways" and in many of the classic movies, including *From Here To Eternity*, *Dr. Zhivago*, and *For Whom the Bell Tolls*. And then there were the wonderful musicals of the 1950's. *The Sound of Music* incorporates a poignant love story, as do *The King and I*, *Brigadoon*, and many others. Even *Lonesome Dove*, Larry McMurtry's classic western novel, contains a love story.

It should come as no surprise, then, that when the Harlequin paperback romance novels were first distributed in the United States some thirty or forty years ago, they became immensely popular with female readers. Harlequin, a Canadian-based publisher, originally gained success in the mid-50's by reprinting romance novels from Mills & Boon, a British publisher who had been publishing romance fiction since 1909. Harlequin purchased Mills & Boon in 1961 and by the early seventies, Harlequin was well-entrenched in the American market.

Janet Dailey was one of those Harlequin romance readers who decided she could write a romance just as well or better than the book she was reading. Challenged by her husband, Bill, to do so, she wrote a romance and sent it off to Harlequin just at the time Harlequin was considering taking on American writers. They bought her book and Janet became the first American author to be published by Harlequin, a feat which opened the door for hundreds of other American romance writers.

It wasn't long until other publishers jumped on the bandwagon and the romance industry soon became like a feeding frenzy for writers and readers.

But, the romance genre has been as fickle at times as some of the early heroines. The early romances were fairly simple. The heroines were sweet, innocent girls who were swept off their feet by strong, masculine men who would take care of them. Eventually, the genre did an about face and the guidelines stressed that the heroine must be strong and independent and that she must tame her man. Eventually, the romance market leveled out and editors became more interested in good stories and good writing than they were formula writing.

Historical and regency romances were as popular as the contemporary romances and since those early days, the romance genre has sprouted subgenres. There are fantasy or paranormal romances, time travel, mystery, suspense, and western romances. There are romances written especially for young adults and those designed to capture the interest of the older reader.

I wasn't a "born writer." I married one. Shortly after Jory Sherman and I were married in 1968, I became his typist and it was during this time that I first had a desire to write a romance. I plotted a romance, but before I could work on it, I was given an opportunity to write a western novel. Jory was writing about ten books a year at the time, including a series of westerns for Zebra Books, when his editor at Zebra asked him to create another western series. They gave him a three-book contract and after writing the first book of the new series, he told me he didn't want to write the series and was going to return the advance he'd received for the two unwritten books. Naive as I was about writing, I offered to write the two remaining books of his contract. He talked to his editor, Leslie Gelbman, and she reluctantly agreed that I could try my hand at writing the books.

I put the romance novel aside and as I wrote that first western, I discovered how hard it was to sit down and actually write a book. With contract renewals, I wrote the next twenty-five books in the Bolt series, with deadlines every other month. During that time, I also wrote four other westerns and by the time the series ended, I was content to be a housewife again.

Oddly enough, it was during a Western Writers of America convention that I made the contact that would lead to the writing of my first romance. Joyce Flaherty, an agent I'd met at a couple of romance conferences, and her husband John, also an agent, attended that WWA convention in Oklahoma City. As Joyce and I renewed our friendship, she encouraged me to get back to writing and before the convention was over, she asked me to write a book for Zebra's new "To Love Again" line.

Elated, I went home and began plotting the story. Joyce had told me that these books were to be about women caught up in the "sandwich generation," women over fifty who had reached that time in their lives when they should be able to relax and enjoy life but who, instead, must be concerned about their elderly parents, their grown children and their grandchildren. While the romance of finding love again was to be the main theme of the book, family relationships were to be explored, too.

It sounded simple enough and I knew that writing a contemporary story had to be easier than writing a book that was set a hundred years ago. While writing the westerns, I relied on Jory, my live-in expert on western history, to help me with the research details. I soon learned, however, that writing a romance took just as much thought and effort as writing in any other genre.

Jory did give me a basic formula for fiction, a formula he has taught to his students over the years that can help with the design of any novel. That premise is as follows: An appealing character struggles against great odds to achieve a worthwhile goal. A romance writer's variation might be stated thusly: A sympathetic heroine seeking change and romance in her life overcomes several obstacles in her journey to find love and happiness in an otherwise dull and frustrating life. The heroine must begin the story with a problem or a series of problems and then begin to take control of her life. In doing so, she will realize her goals and find fulfillment as a woman with a man of her dreams.

Write about what you know. That's the advice I'd heard often enough at writers' conferences. Knowing that I wanted to include an Ozarks setting in my book, I gave my heroine a plush Coachman motor home like the one we used to have, which she would drive across the country by herself from her home in Montana to Branson, Missouri, where she would join up with other campers who were attending an RV rally.

I sent off the plot summary and ran right square into my first stumbling block. The editor liked the story line and asked me to write the first three chapters, but it seems the publisher considered campers to be a lower class people than she wanted portrayed in her books. And, I was talking about a motor home in the fifty to sixty thousand dollar price range!

Determined to write the book, I read a few current romance novels to refresh myself on the writing style of romances, then wrote the first four chapters of the book and sent them off. I finally got a contract, along with a letter from my editor stating that these books were not to be written like romances, but were to be written like mainstream novels. So I started over again, relieved that I didn't have to use the purple prose and sexual euphemisms that had become the trademarks of the early romances.

The first two or three chapters are the hardest to write, I think, but by chapter four, I was so caught up in the story I ignored all household chores. When my heroine finally arrived in the Ozarks in her motor home, I felt more at home. It was as if I were seeing the beauty of these Ozarks hills for the first time through her eyes. I managed to steer her away from the hustle and bustle of the tourist attractions and guide her through the awesome scenery of the woods and lakes.

Halfway through the writing of the book, I took two days off to attend an overnight get-together with a few of my writer friends. In discussing our current projects, one of the other women said she hoped I had a good villain in my book because she liked villains. My heart sank. I didn't have a villain in my book, I realized. When I got home and read through the pages I'd written, I spotted the character who was the obvious villain. I strengthened his character, then had to rein him in as he began to take over the story. Another stumbling block overcome.

As I was writing the last chapter in the book, I began to feel the pressure of the approaching deadline ease somewhat. That's when I got another letter from my editor which said the new title of my book was *A Kiss at Sunrise*, changed from my working title of *Autumn Sunset*. She had drawn a little happy face near the new title. I didn't mind the change, in fact, I'd expected one. But, a kiss at sunrise? There was no such scene in my book. So, I quickly scanned through the chapters on my computer screen and found a logical place where my hero and heroine could share a kiss as they watched the sun rise over the lake at a wooded campground.

With that scene added, I finally finished the last chapter and sent the manuscript off to my editor. I had accomplished my dream of some twenty years to write a romance. But, more important, I learned a lot about writing. I discovered that writing a romance was not that much different from writing a western. A different time frame, yes, but the characters and the story line are what count.

When I was asked to write a short story for a Christmas collection for the same "To Love Again" line, I chose an Ozarks setting again. This time I placed the older heroine in a secluded log cabin that she'd inherited from her grandparents, avoiding the glitter of Branson. I wanted to create a feeling of loneliness because, with her grown children in other parts of the country, my widowed heroine had to face the fact that she would be spending Christmas all alone for the first time in her life. The serenity of the quiet winter woods worked for this story.

Then my editor asked me to write a romance set in the Branson music scene. This was a challenge for me. There's a mystical quality to the woods and the hills around here that I like to explore in my books and yet I knew I had to plunge my characters into the heart of the entertainment world here in Branson. I gave my heroine the occupation of entertainment editor for the local paper so she'd be knowledgeable about the music business. Her love interest was a once-popular singer who came to Branson to make a comeback in his career. I modeled him after my friend, country singer Tommy

Overstreet, and studied Tommy's picture as I described my character's beautiful silver-gray hair, his moustache and neatly trimmed beard.

With my characters in place, including a villain this time, I was able to give the story the flavor of the music scene by creating a fictional musical theater with all its vibrancy and flare, and by mentioning the names of several of the top-name entertainers who perform in Branson. But, I also managed to work in the feel of the Ozarks by contrasting the glitz of the strip with the serenity of the nearby woods and lakes and secluded fishing coves. And, through dialogue, I covered some of the history of the area and told how the music industry started in Branson nearly fifty years ago.

At some point during the writing, I received the letter I'd been expecting from my editor telling me that the title of my book had been changed to *Country Lovesong*, which was a better title than I had used.

With a sign of relief, I finally typed "The End" and spent the day printing out the manuscript. No sooner was that done than I received an overnight express letter from my editor informing me that they had already taken the picture for the front cover of my book and that I would have to make a few changes because the hero now had dark brown hair and was clean shaven and the heroine had shoulder-length hair instead of a short bob.

After taking a few deep breaths and thinking a few words I didn't say aloud, I turned the computer back on and got to work. It would have been simple to make the changes if I could have used the search and replace feature of the computer, but I had to read through every one of the 440 pages. I had given the hero the trait of scratching his beard when he was deep in thought and I had to be sure that I removed all traces of his beard and his gray hair.

With the changes made, I printed the entire manuscript

again and after I mailed it, I kicked off my shoes and took the rest of the day off, ignoring the dirty dishes that had stacked up during the two frantic days it had taken me to make the changes.

I just finished reading the galley proofs a few days before writing this chapter and noticed that most of the history of the area had been cut out. The editor was probably right in this case. This is a romance novel, after all, and I had included the historical material because I was curious enough about the beginning of the music industry in Branson to do the research.

Maybe I'll write an historical romance one of these days and if I do, I'll set it in these Ozark hills. I already have all the research I need.

Veda Boyd Jones

Veda Boyd Jones has published over one hundred magazine articles and stories in a variety of magazines, including *Writer's Digest*, *Highlights for Children*, *Country America*, and *American Farm and Home Almanac*.

Since 1991 she has published seven romance novels, including *Callie's Challenge*. *The Secret of the Halloween Fires*, her first children's book, is a 1995 release from Story Factory.

Jones was born in Sulphur Springs, Arkansas and currently lives in Joplin, Missouri, with her architect husband and three sons.

Writing the Inspirational Romance

I wasn't one of those people who knew from second grade that I wanted to be a writer. Although I edited the newspaper in high school and junior college, I didn't consciously think about being a writer and certainly not about writing anything remotely inspirational. My writing came as a result of needing a sense of accomplishment just for me.

In 1981 my husband Jim and I moved our family to Tulsa, Oklahoma, where he had a job with an architectural firm. By the end of the second day in our new home, we were unpacked. On the third day, I found the public library and enrolled our oldest son in story hour.

I couldn't get a library card. Like most city libraries, the policy was for the borrower to show proof of residency. I didn't have printed checks yet or mail delivered to our new address. All I could do was take some paperback books on the honor system. My choice was limited to romances and westerns. I chose romances.

Not knowing anyone in Tulsa, I dialed the time and temperature number just so I could use the phone. During the day I played with our sons, kept house, and read.

One night, after Jim and the boys were in bed, I finished a romance I had started earlier. I read the last page, put down the book, and said "I can do better than that." It was raining – actually it was a dark and stormy night. And as I listened to the rain pelt the roof, I wondered how someone wrote a book. How could a writer keep the characters going through two hundred pages?

I read more romances, even though I now had a card at the library, and I decided to write one. For two weeks I plotted. I'd write what I knew. My hero would be an architect (Jim) and the heroine would be a historian (I have a master's degree in history). I wrote character sketches, using the little knowledge I had gained from my creative writing class in college years earlier.

I started my new career as a writer during the boys' nap time on March 1, 1982, which was a Monday. New month, new day of the week – somehow it seemed ideal. I wrote on the typewriter and finished the book after we moved to Joplin where Jim was offered a partnership in a firm. I revised the book once. Then I typed it over, which took five months of naps.

The book was rejected by Harlequin a week after our third son was born. At the time I thought it was a form rejection even though it had my name on the letter. My plot needed to be flushed out. If I wanted to revise the manuscript, they'd take another look at it. Of course, I thought that was their standard way of saying no, thanks. I stuck the manuscript in a drawer.

I had read several of Jessica Steele's Harlequin romance novels and discovered that it was her seventh manuscript that sold. So, I decided to write seven romances before I gave up. Why would I think I was a better writer than Steele?

I started my next romance. I was only a few chapters

into it when our family went to North Carolina on vacation. We were joining some friends, Cathy and Bill, at Cathy's parents' cabin in the mountains. Cathy had read my first romance manuscript and asked that I bring what I had of the second.

The cabin turned out to be a house twice the size of my house and located on an exclusive mountain with a guard at the gate. Obviously Cathy's family had money.

Cathy read my several chapters. Her mother, who had written and sold confession stories years earlier, asked if she could read them. I was flattered and said yes.

"What's your conflict?" she asked when she finished.

"There's no conflict," I replied. "They're just dating. It's a romance."

There still needs to be something to keep them apart," she said. "You need to take a writing class."

I smiled, but didn't look her in the eye. Who did she think she was telling me, someone who had written a master's thesis, that I needed to take a writing class? I swallowed my anger. After all, I was staying at her house.

"I'll think about it," I said.

Back in Missouri I wrote her a thank you note for her hospitality and received a note from her in return mail:

"I believe you have writing talent, but you need to hone your skills. I'm willing to pay for you to take a writing class, up to $500."

I was still furious, as new writers are when their work is criticized, and I decided to call her bluff. Although $500 was a lot of money to me, I knew it wouldn't strain her financially. I checked into our local college writing course, but it was on poetry and essays and not geared toward commercial writing. I opted for a correspondence course for a couple hundred dollars.

I learned from that course. I learned about conflict and

theme, point of view, and sentence variety. And I kept writing.

My second romance was rejected, and my third, and my fourth. By now I knew it would be hard to sell a book, but I wasn't discouraged because I had discovered magazine markets, both for children and adults. I began selling articles and short stories, and finally that MA in history paid off. I had the credentials to write for reference books. These sales kept me going as I wrote on another romance manuscript.

I had also discovered networking. I had joined the Joplin Writers' Guild and attended an Ozark Writers League meeting with a friend. There I met an Avalon editor who bought my first romance. *April's Autumn* was the fifth book manuscript I'd written, but the first I'd written on the computer. It had been revised and revised without retyping. Although set in Colorado, the heroine April was an Arkansas native who missed an Ozark autumn – thus the title, which was picked by the editor, not by me.

With my foot in the door, I wrote another romance for Avalon, which published squeaky-clean hardback romances for the library market. The editor read the first chapter and outline and said write the book. I did. She called and said it was too mainstream, not enough romance. Try again.

I sent her another proposal. Write it, she said. I did. She called and said it was too episodic. Try again.

I sent her a third proposal, this time a version of the first manuscript I'd ever written. Write it, she said. I did. She called and said I couldn't plot.

Discouraged? Me? You bet! I felt like a dog that had been kicked. Obviously I couldn't write. *April's Autumn* was a fluke.

What could I do with three squeaky-clean romances? They didn't fit with the sexual chemistry needed for a Harlequin or Silhouette. A friend suggested I try the inspirational market.

At first I resisted, not knowing how to attempt it, although I checked the bookstores for Christian romances. Historical romances filled the shelves, but I didn't find one contemporary.

My friend persisted. Surely there was a publisher who was looking for my type of book. Giving into her badgering, I borrowed a Christian writer's market book and sent off three chapters and a synopsis to several publishers. My proposals came back in return mail, rejected because they weren't historical. I tried a couple more publishers.

An editor called from Barbour Books. They were just starting a new line of romances called Heartsong Presents for a book club and were looking for books. He liked my three chapters. Did the book have religion in it?

"No, but it's clean," I said. "No sex."

"We need a Christian background for our novels. Can you add it?" he asked.

"Of course," I said with much more confidence than I was feeling.

I worked on the manuscript, not adding a conversion story or a heavy-handed message, but adding beliefs that confirmed my own values.

He sent a contract.

Gentle Persuasion was the book that the other editor had said was too mainstream. By adding a religious conflict and strengthening the romance angle, I had a better book.

Set in a fictitious Missouri town that resembled Neosho, Missouri, where I'd gone to high school, *Gentle Persuasion*, reflected my thoughts on baseball. I portrayed life in a small Ozark town where community members express their views and take sides on issues. In this novel, an English teacher's stance against adding baseball to the high school sports roster is challenged by an injury-retired major league baseball pitcher. Both hero and heroine learn the gentle art of compromise.

I was thrilled with the success of my first Christian romance. Could I do it again?

I took the episodic romance and added a Christian inner conflict for the heroine. In *Under a Texas Sky*, a movie is being made at the ruins of old Fort Phantom Hill near Abilene. The heroine gets involved with a screenwriter and the excitement of movie making. She doesn't want to reveal that she's a Christian to the Hollywood set. The hero teaches her that she doesn't have to say anything about religion, that her Christian beliefs speak for themselves in the way she treats other people. It wasn't preachy, just an easy-going message. The Christian message made the book stronger.

Next I looked at the second manuscript I'd ever written, *The Governor's Daughter*. This was the one I'd taken to North Carolina several years earlier. It had been written on the typewriter and was aimed at the Silhouette market. I revised extensively as I input it into the computer. The spiritual message was one of the power of prayer and learning to trust those we love. I dedicated it to that woman in North Carolina who had paid for my writing course.

I used Fayetteville, Arkansas, and the University as my setting. I went to school there, so I knew the layout and the atmosphere of an Ozark college campus.

Did my editor settle for second best because these books had been rejected before? I don't think so. On the basis of those three books, the readers at Heartsong Presents voted me one of their favorite authors. And in the end, it's the readers' verdict that counts.

I've learned not to give up on a manuscript that I believe in. Although it may be rejected, I let it sit, then work on it again. I evaluate any criticism that an editor offers, and if I feel it merits attention, I revise the manuscript to alleviate the problem.

My next book for Heartsong Presents was *A Sign of Love*, that first manuscript I wrote about the architect and the historian. I had rewritten it for Avalon, and now I took a serious look at why that editor had felt it was badly plotted. I took out scenes that didn't further the story and paid strict attention to the conflict. I let the hero and heroine learn to compromise and complement each other's opposite views. The Christian message in this one was for the hero, Grant, to be less judgmental and decide he needed to be in church even though he felt it was filled with hypocrites.

The setting was again in Arkansas; this time in a fictitious small town called Butler Creek, but set about where Harrison is. I let the characters travel to Branson, Missouri and wrote about the heavy traffic and entertainment industry of that area. I also let the land – the caves, the streams, and the hills – play a part in the book.

Callie's Mountain was another early manuscript that I revised. Although it's set in the mountains of North Carolina (I only write about places I've been), I used my knowledge of Ozark people and my relatives in Arkansas to create the character of Grandma, who is central to the story. She is a strong woman, God-fearing, honest, and cantankerous.

"Year-rounders and summer people don't mix." she says time and time again, reestablishing the differences in the haves and have-nots.

Grandma tells Callie, whose mother died in childbirth, that her father isn't dead. He was a wealthy summer person, and Grandma doesn't know his last mane. Callie decides to find him and learn of her heritage. The Christian message in this novel is forgiveness. Again, it isn't heavy-handed, just a theme woven around Callie's search for identity.

The sequel, *Callie's Challenge*, continues the theme of forgiveness.

Christian historical romances lean toward conversion stories. A Christian-frontier-woman-leads-a-man-to-the-right-path type of story. There are several Christian publishers who buy historicals. This type of book has a longer shelf life than contemporary inspirational romances. Details quickly date a contemporary novel. Five years ago a heroine might mention putting a cassette in the player. Now she'd use a CD.

Contemporary Christian romances currently have only two publishers, Heartsong Presents by Barbour Books and Palisade Romance by Questar Publishers. With the success of contemporary romances in book clubs and Christian book stores, the list is bound to grow.

Although the guidelines for inspirational romances are fairly rigid compared to their secular counterpart (no drinking, no smoking, no sex, no cussing, no dancing, no divorce, modest clothing), it's not difficult to fit characters into this line of thinking by avoiding the settings that usually prompt frowned-upon activities. The main characters must be strong and believable, and interact within this framework, and have a strong belief (at least by the end of the book) in God.

Christian characters aren't all pure and honest. The characters make real choices to real problems all of us face and have to live with their choices. They have flaws in their personalities, just like all good characters. Learning to overcome those flaws, with God's help, is an important part of the book.

The underlying theme is that a strong religious belief (no doctrine outlined at all) is the cornerstone for a happy-ever-after relationship between a man and a woman. Is passion missing from these romances? Not at all. Love triumphs and is made stronger by a Christian basis.

Occasionally I've used church settings to get a Christian message across, normally having the minister's sermon fit nicely into what's going on in the characters' lives.

These are not preachy books, so I don't spend a whole page giving a sermon. I dwell on what reaction the character has to what she's heard in church.

Settings both in the United States and abroad are popular among inspirational readers. While plotting my next romance, I asked the editor if any one region received a better response from the readers. He saw none. However, he thought I should use what I know best.

"Our readers are always interested in the Ozarks," he said. "And you know the land and the people. Use them."

I will.

Charlie Farmer

Charlie Farmer has been a full-time professional writer, specializing in first-hand outdoor adventure magazine articles and books since 1969. He has lived in Ozark, Missouri for nineteen years. In 1988 Farmer was named The Conservation Communicator of the Year by the Conservation Federation of Missouri for his outstanding contribution to the wise use of our nation's resources.

He has written ten books about fishing, hunting, camping, canoeing, backpacking, and outdoor cooking. Farmer's outdoor and conservation columns appear weekly in the *Springfield* [Missouri] *News-Leader* and *St. Louis Labor Tribune*. He also co-hosts a weekly outdoor radio program in Springfield, Missouri, called the Outside Story.

Writing About Outdoor Adventure

As of July, 1995, I have been full-time freelance writing for 26 consecutive years. I began this fantastic adventure into the unknown at age 25, still a bachelor and brimming with unabashed cockiness and strong measure of reckless optimism. Seeking the opinions of close writer associates at the Wyoming Game and Fish Department where I worked in 1969, I informed them about the idea of striking off on my own as an independent scribe, trotting the globe in search of Hemingway trout streams and Zane Grey bluewater billfish. There was no doubt in my mind that if Ernest and Zane broke fertile ground as outdoor writers, I could follow their tracks.

My closest associate, fifteen years older than I, was a fine editor, writer, and photographer who I greatly admired. His opinion was vital. But when I asked him about leaving my state job and flying on my own, his answer jolted me like the kick of a 375 H & H Magnum.

He puffed softly on his pipe before answering, as though he himself had long debated this very career option within the chambers of his own mind. After all, to me he was the ultimate pro who commanded an argosy of adventure words and settings second to none. With characteristic softness in his mellow voice, in between long draws of Forest Blend pipe tobacco, he finally answered, "You are treading on perilous ground with this freelancing thing. I've thought about it myself. Lord knows I have freelanced enough stuff to the men's magazines. But quitting a real job and doing it everyday scares the hell out of me."

He paused and looked into my eyes. I could almost feel his words hit home before he spoke. "You're a young guy. You need more experiences. Why don't you freelance on the side for a while? Get to know a few editors and make a name for yourself."

Two weeks later I handed in my resignation. I had $7,000 in the bank and vowed that I would give it one full year to see if I had what it takes to call myself a bonafide, independent writer. If at the end of the year I was still ticking and had any money left, I'd go for another.

In order to claim full-time writer status that first year I transcended the narrow boundaries of outdoor writing and queried magazines of all sizes and descriptions. *The Writer's Market* was the book I lived by. At first, I sought out not the largest, most prestigious publications, but the ones whose guidelines seemed to encourage first-time contributors.

Along with *Fur Fish & Game* and the NRA's new magazine, *The American Hunter*, I sold $35 and $40 pieces to the *National Shoe Reporter* and the *American Milk Journal* among other trade books. Trained as a newspaper reporter in college, I was taught to investigate, research and write about any topic that was assigned. Although my overwhelming preference was outdoor adventure, initially, the subject matter was of little significance as long as I was writing full-time.

I saw little difference between researching the retail shoe business or new techniques in mechanized dairy farming. I measured each check as a bite out of the rent payment here and a week's worth of groceries there. Mostly pay on publication checks, the money seemed slow in coming and for three months I dipped grudgingly into my savings. But progress was being made.

As long as I can remember, probably from age five, I had this burning desire to fish and hunt. There is nothing abnormal about this except that I grew up in the Bronx, New York, fairly well removed from anything that even remotely resembled a duck marsh or trout stream. My dad was not a hunter or angler, but he was born in Scotland and maybe somewhere along the gene trail I was meant to be a sportsman. The love of outdoor sport and adventure has never dwindled. More than anything, this is why I have achieved a smattering of success.

As a kid growing up in the city, my wilderness adventures were contained within the pages of the "Big Three" outdoor magazines – *Field & Stream*, *Outdoor Life* and *Sports Afield.* When magazine editorial requirements recommended becoming familiar with the contents and style of writing, I unknowingly got a tremendous jump. I devoured fishing, hunting and camping articles as though my life depended on them. I was gleaning information for the time when I could strike out to woods and waters. Little did I know then, in the initial, vicarious process of becoming an outdoorsman, I was also honing future writing skills.

The first year was a good one and I counted that as proof that my decision to freelance was sound. In addition to a dozen or so small, steady markets, I struck pay dirt with first-submission feature sales to *Field & Stream*, *Outdoor Life* and *Sports Afield* all within a three month period.

The glory days of "Me and Joe" outdoor writing, the 1950s, 1960s, and 1970s, were still blooming when I made my start in 1969. I was fortunate that the magazines and their editors still worked by a fair code of ethics and professionalism in their treatment of writers. One particular editor, Bill Rae, *Outdoor Life*'s editor from 1950 until 1973, was one of the best. So was Jack Samson of *Field & Stream* and Ted Kesting of *Sports Afield.* Whether the generic, depersonalized rejection form had been invented yet, I don't know. But Rae, Samson, Kesting, Bert Darga and Gene Hill, did not use them.

From all appearances, Bill Rae typed his own letters of rejection or acceptance. It is never easy to accept the former, but with Rae's personal interest, even the sour notes were somewhat palatable. When he said "no" to a query or manuscript, he spent at least three or four paragraphs explaining why. Some of those rejections had favorable loop holes such as, "If you can supply a few more anecdotes, add some bighorn sheep biology with an interview or two, and tighten up the writing a bit, I'll take another look at it."

This was wholesome incentive in its purest form. Bill Rae, an editor from New York, who I never met, taught me to become a better, more persistent writer. The turn-around time for query letters and buy-on speculation manuscripts ranged between two and three weeks. Oh, the good old days!

The late 1970s was a transition period for outdoor writing. Those who had been in the business much longer than I, seasoned pros like Erwin A. Bauer, Col. Dave Harbour, and Byron Dalyrymple sensed the change. Old guard gentlemen editors were gradually being replaced by new-breed executive types who out of necessity were more corporate driven than their predecessors. Erwin Bauer told me in the Jackson, Wyoming, post office one day that drastic changes were in store for fulltime freelancers. He said it would be difficult starting out now. Bauer and I aggreed that the new emphasis on "how-to, where-to and hot-spotting" articles instead of first-person yarn spinning, would produce a formula-writing, ever-growing generation of outdoor reporters.

"Everybody that owns a Nikon will get into the outdoor writing field," he predicted.

Changes occurred quickly. Competition for features in major magazines grew intense. Nobody wanted me and Joe anymore. An already favorable buyers' market became more so. Editors were deluged with queries, manuscripts and photography. Printed rejection slips and stamped editorial signatures replaced personalized notes and the turn-around time for submissions changed from weeks to months to sometimes never.

The "Big Three" magazines, desperately trying to reach a more sophisticated generation of outdoorsmen, sought new identities using slick graphics, revamped covers and fresh how-to writers. For a while, I felt that Bauer had painted too much of a doomsday portrait of the business. But as the 1980s blossomed, outdoor writing emerged as a hardcore stereotype of "biggest horns, longest beards, record fish, tournament tactics and secret hot-spots." Storytelling was lost in the shuffle.

During this time, a new crop of narrowly focused specialty and regional outdoor magazines were born, further diluting the once-fabled strength of the Big Three. Created were magazines for every species of fish, game, brand of sport, product and conservation cause. Some lasted a year or two, others retained a strong enough bite on the market to survive. Most are pay on publication books that purchase feature materials for $300 or less.

When it comes to payment, outdoor magazines have held steady or lowered rates since 1970. Granted, some established authors may pick up an extra $100 over the standard. Outdoor publishers know however, that there is a never-ending supply of fishing and hunting writers or part-timers out there who are not as concerned about pay as they are about seeing their names in print. Enough of those writers submit acceptable formula manuscripts and pictures to keep competition among part-timers and pros fierce. Staff and field writers for specific magazines get an economic boost now and then. But the freelancer trying to make a living covering a variety of publications must be content with current, suppressed rates or else move on to another career or brand of writing.

Feeble attempts to raise magazine and newspaper rates have surfaced periodically within the Outdoor Writers Association of America (OWAA) over the past 20 years. An organization of 2,000 writers, editors, lecturers, photographers, artists, filmmakers, radio and television broadcasters who communicate the outdoor experiences to the public, OWAA does not claim to be a guild bent on obtaining cost-of-living wages for its members. The loose association of full-time and part-time communicators, founded in 1927, prevents that mission.

A core of full-timers, this writer included, tried to consolidate a fee-bargaining network within the association several years ago. Completely unsuccessful, it served to do nothing but alienate most of the membership who do not make their living writing full-time. Opponents within the ranks called us elitist trouble makers. They worried that we would upset current relations with editors and publishers and make the situation even worse than it was. As negotiators, we faded into the sunset.

The bottom line is that if every well-established full-time writer in OWAA banded together, struck and held out for higher wages, all of us would be out of work. Publishers and editors could round-up replacements in a day and there is no way those substitutes would be called scabs. Air traffic controllers believed they had clout. For sure, bargaining-wise, they have significantly more than freelance outdoor writers. Their fate is documented. Doctors, lawyers, architects, engineers, chemists, pharmacists and California screen writers have clout.

In all fairness to OWAA, and I have been an active member since 1969, the association's value is derived from its annual conference, workshops, seminars, guest speakers and monthly newsletter, *Outdoors Unlimited*. The social bounty of this fraternity alone, getting together with others of similar outdoor and writing passion, is worth every penny of the $100 annual dues. (OWAA, 2017 Cato Ave., Suite 101, State College, PA 16801-2768 (800) 692-2477)

If the pay per hour and net profit is hideously low in relation to expenses, time spent researching and writing a speculation-submitted outdoor adventure feature, and the economics of the business is not likely to change in the near future, why stay? How many thousands of writers in all specialized fields of craft ask themselves the same question.

Simply put, it's because we are writers and need to write. If we strike gold, fine. If we don't, we move ahead in hopes of spawning immortal words – in my case the outdoor adventure that positively changes the lives of one or more readers. What more could a writer ask for other than some money to live on. All writers are gifted, some more than others. I am proud to call myself a writer.

"Geez, how does it feel to have the greatest job in the world?" they ask me. "You fish, hunt, and camp around the world and get paid for it. You're the boss. Work at home. No eight to five. Where do I sign up?"

These are the words I most frequently hear from friends and strangers alike when commenting on my occupation. "Terrific," I say half tongue and cheek, knowing full well that surely these office workers, laborers and university students realize the occupation has monstrous pitfalls. I want to tell them that they can do the same by writing good stories from early morning to late afternoon each day, whether they feel like writing or not. And if they don't mind eating, sleeping, recreating and working in the same house everyday, their chances of doing what I do are good.

But it does make me stop and think about what I do and the fact that very few others in the world do it full-time. Good and bad mental responses stem from this question. "My extraordinary writing skills, discipline and persistence make it possible. Or, I'm one of the few crazy enough to think they can pursue and make a living as a freelance outdoor writer."

The more inquisitive types ask me if I can really make a living writing about outdoor adventure sports. It's a bold question that sometimes makes me want to shoot back, "Can you really make a living being a lawyer these days? Is my economic situation really any business of yours?" But I mellow and realize that they ask out of honest curiosity about an occupation that is intriguing. And that they may never have met a real writer before. After all, how many full-time writers do you have on your block or on your over-forty softball team?

I tell them I can and do make a living pursuing outdoor adventure. And when I feel that their curiosity is genuine, I respond by saying that in order to survive and sometimes flourish in the outdoor writing field a writer has to be more than a writer.

The heyday of tucking oneself into a pine shrouded log cabin, and churning out first-person adventure stories are generally considered dreams of the past. That pipe-smoking recluse of yesteryear may have been an outdoor writer in the purest sense of the word. God knows we all strive for literary purity – a commitment to good magazines, books, or both. It was easier in the glory days to find a singular niche and make a fair living from it.

Today, most full-time outdoor writers diversify into the total spectrum of communication. When the days of outdoor writing's wine and roses ebbed in the late 1970s, those who made adjustments survived. Others, some top names and fine writers, called it quits. My own transition was difficult. I was nudged out of the log cabin in Wyoming and forced to try things that scared me to death.

After twenty-six years of outdoor writing, I'm still in the diversification mode. Anything that keeps me writing, creating and getting outdoors is worth the effort. Not meaning to gloat, because there are outdoor writers far more successful than I, here's what I do to survive and have some fun out of life in the process. There are no secrets withheld.

Ten outdoor adventure books published. Editorial and photo credits in major magazines including "The Big Three", *National Geographic*, and a variety of camping, boating and general consumer magazines. Weekly outdoor columns in two major newspapers. Regular sales of outdoor action color and black and white photos from a file stock of over 50,000 photographs. Weekly outdoor radio program. Instructional video production, on-air host, script writing and consulting. Television script writing, commercials, on-air hosting and consulting. Regular public speaking and production of slide show, seminars, lunch and after dinner talks. And freelance public relations consultant, newsletter design, copy writing and editing, news releases and brochures. As of this writing, while carrying on my weekly and monthly assignments, I am working on my eleventh outdoor book. And by no means am I the only outdoor writer covering all bases in the communication field.

Fifteen years ago public speaking terrified me. The instructional video tape market had not yet arrived and the last thing I wanted to do was get involved in television, radio and public relations. I had prided myself on being pure writer.

In 26 years of freelancing I have never lost my love or desire to write about the outdoors, conservation and nature, but I have, during that span, suffered through several bouts of burnout. It was never caused by lack of story ideas. I write down at least 10 new story and book ideas every week. The burnout came from spending too much time in front of the typewriter and computer trying to make a decent living. It reached the point that some of my neighbors were doing more fishing, hunting and camping than I was.

It was during this time period when I knew I had to make some changes or else look for a dreaded office job. That thought scared me. While there are always unpredictable peaks and valleys for full-time writers, diversification and reaching out beyond the walls of my office not only paid off with extra income, but added change-of-pace variety to weekly assignments. Blended into magazine, book and newspaper columns, the additions of radio, television, video, public speaking and public relations have been for the most part pleasurable.

Some magazine and book writers have the skills, savvy and good fortune to survive without diversification. But in the outdoor field today, their numbers are few. And it is true that some others, who may need the extra commercial work, do not have the personality or talents to branch out. Writers trying to make it full-time today, supporting themselves and possibly a family, will have a difficult time surviving in the business without being versatile. College courses in all areas of printed and electronic media communications can help make the transition easier for a newcomer or seasoned writer.

Most outdoor writers today cannot afford to hire an agent or public relations firm to represent them. The majority of agents know very little about specialty outdoor magazine and book writing. For this reason, it is essential for a writer to learn self-marketing skills. A writer's letterhead, correspondence, resume, community involvement, awards and accomplishments should be displayed and promoted stylishly and often. Getting out and making important contacts through writers' groups and professional organizations are steps in the right direction. Self-produced news releases and quality author portraits produced by professional photo studios, are just some of the marketing tools available to the freelancers.

Writers, by their nature, are often solitary introverts who have a difficult time promoting their talents. If each of us wrote best selling books from the confines of our home office, self-promotion would not matter much. Our publishers would take care of that. Otherwise, those without best selling books, should yield to the fact that when you don't promote yourself in a professional manner, no one else will.

Despite our freedom from office drudgery, clock punching, clock watching, dress codes and over-the-shoulder bosses, today's independent writer, regardless of specialty subject matter, needs to place greater emphasis on sound business practices than ever before. Claiming that being "too business oriented" interferes with or stifles virgin creativity, is no longer a valid excuse. Working writers must know and honestly evaluate the economic results of writing projects beforehand. Most of us have a difficult, if not impossible time, turning down assignments. Our bargaining power is minimal. We can still write from the heart, but we must also be able to justify or reject a twenty-hour writing assignment that pays $200, not counting research time, travel and phone expenses.

Outdoor writers, myself included, generally have a bumpkin-like reputation when it comes to financial justification of many of the jobs we choose to accept. We end up doing things for the glory of outdoor adventure and the spirit of rugged individualism when we should be thinking whether the money earned will be enough to cover next month's mortgage payment.

It wasn't until I turned fifty that I began thinking more about the realities of just compensation. As free spirits, we outdoor writers tend to coast financially as long as we can do our thing. Times have changed. During my first year freelancing in Wyoming, I lived on moose, elk, antelope, deer, duck, rabbit and trout flesh to save money. I savored that pioneering spirit. Today, big game meat is not as available to me as it once was. Most of my groceries come from the supermarket.

Because of exposure in magazines and newspaper columns, outdoor writers are frequently asked to give talks and slide shows to sportsmen, business and civic groups. For several years I had this hangup about charging a speaker's fee. I figured selling some of my books at these talks would provide enough compensation.

However, as I discovered later, the success of books sales vary depending on the audience and time allotted. A combination thirty-minute talk and slide presentation, tailored to a specific group, takes about eight hours worth of preparation. Digging out appropriate slides is the most time consuming phase of the assignment.

Two years ago, because of an increasing number of invitations to speak, I decided in the name of sensible business, to start charging a fee. Most requests come by phone and the most awkward situations for me, after being complimented by the caller with a glowing invitation to speak, was informing that person of my fee. Some organizations were willing to pay, others could not. Now, rather than feeling bad about it, I accept the arrangement as part of doing business. Considering preparation and actual speaking time, the margin of profit is slim, but it helps. I still present some talks and seminars free to charitable groups.

Outdoor adventure writing opportunities for me have expanded from "hook and bullet" articles and books to non-consumptive sports such as camping, hiking, backpacking, cycling, canoeing, boating, nature photography and conservation issues. While fishing and hunting is still my bread and butter, the other options are exciting and offer pleasing variations to the basic list of topics I cover. Writing versatility has helped me survive.

There are successful outdoor writers who specialize in singular topics such as fly fishing, bass fishing, deer hunting or upland game bird hunting, but because I have enjoyed all phases of outdoor sport, my preference is covering the gamut. While I have done a significant number of personality articles and research stories, my trademark is getting out there, doing it by myself, with relatives, friends or with established experts, then writing about it.

Unlike most general magazine and newspaper reporters, the successful outdoor writer achieves a degree of proficiency in adventure sports that is conveyed in first-person style to the readers. In my opinion, an outdoor writer who is not an active participant and strictly a research interviewer, lacks the editorial emotion and authenticity necessary to convey material and photographs in a believable, entertaining manner.

Regarding photos, both color and black and white, an outdoor writer who professionally illustrates his own articles and books, or those of other writers, is ten steps ahead of his competitors. In the process, articles and books become more attractive products to editors when they are enhanced with good photography. Packing cameras and shooting pictures when fish are biting furiously and ducks are pouring into the decoys, takes discipline, but the efforts increase a writer's earning power.

Today's compact single lens reflex (SLR) cameras are relatively inexpensive and simple to use. The best photographic tip is to pack a camera wherever you go. A mini-35 millimeter point and shoot camera, carried in a belt pouch and ready when you are, captures fast breaking action that commonly occurs outdoors when you least expect it.

Outdoor writers who survive in the business have a work ethic that astonishes most people who outwardly believe the "job" is cushy and can be performed by just about anybody. For starters, the writer-sportsman has to be in good enough physical shape to enjoy and withstand the rigors of dawn to dusk adventure. This could be a backpack elk hunting trip to Wyoming or a cold-blasted December day in Missouri hunting ducks and geese.

In order to obtain fresh, original story material, an outdoor writer needs to plan, travel, and actively participate in rigorous and sometimes dangerous outdoor sports on a regular basis. Then, when the adventures are completed, head back to the office and carefully convey the sights, sounds, smells, feels, success, failure and emotions of the experience. The most difficult part of outdoor writing for most of us, is doing what we love outdoors and then having to come home, cloister ourselves indoors and duplicate the adventure on paper. An outdoor writer indoors is a fish out of water. And the pain of not being "out" there is always hard to bear.

Most of all, the successful writer must possess a burning love for nature, the outdoors, and outdoor adventure of all kinds. It is only outdoors that an outdoor writer truly comes alive.

There are pitfalls in the business and inexperienced writers sometimes fall into them. I did. One is the offer of glamorous trips to all parts of the world by persons and companies that would benefit by a well-placed magazine or newspaper article mentioning a certain resort, outfitter, state town, or product.

Exciting stories and pictures commonly result from these offers. Most outdoor adventure hosts are legitimate. But the final ethical and financial decision belongs to the writer alone. Economically justifying a two week snowmobiling trip to Iceland to make a single, $300 dollar sale to a specialty magazine is hard to do. But in the spirit of adventure and a once-in-a-lifetime trip, what inquisitive writer-type could turn such an invitation down?

Of more serious ethical concern when accepting hosted adventure trips is being honest with yourself and your prospective host. Whether the host stipulates it or not, you need legitimate markets for the story lined up before you make a commitment. Some outdoor recreation vendors require that writers have assignments from reputable magazines or newspapers before adventure trips and expenses are offered. Ideally, a magazine or newspaper editor assigns a staff writer or freelancer the story. Even then, as outdoor and travel writers are well aware, the writer is ethically responsible for story truth and accuracy. If a trip goes sour or does not live up to the billing of host sponsors, a potential published story may have to be sacrificed for the sake of honesty.

Some trips go that way. A full-time freelance writer should always make it clear up front to a host that there are no guarantees that the story will be published. And, of course, any writer worth his salt does not want to spend ten days or so without bagging at least one or two stories to economically justify the trip.

Writers get into ethical and financial trouble when they interpret material gathering trips as free vacations with no obligations attached.

There are other pitfalls and I have experienced most of them in twenty-six years. Self-pity, loneliness, no office

Christmas parties, unpredictable paychecks and the never-ending procession of deadlines are some of the more common ones. These are temporary setbacks. Remember, the outdoor writer has the greatest job in the world, even if he is poor. You can still have a social life if you are disciplined to write eight to five every day. Actually, you can live quite a normal life if that's what you want.

As far as the future is concerned for outdoor writers, there cannot be a more exciting time than now. In a hectic world of chaos and grinding daily routine, we writers give our audiences a chance to escape into nature. We introduce them to healthy, adventurous lifestyles. And we present them tranquility and hope. There is no pill or magic potion that can offer the same. We should be proud!

Ellen Gray Massey

Ellen Gray Massey is the author of numerous short stories, articles, and books. Since 1991, she has published five novels for the Avalon imprint of Thomas Bouregy & Company of New York.

In addition to writing books, she has served as editor for two others, *Bittersweet County* and *Bittersweet Earth,* and two periodicals.

Her stories and novels have won her several awards and recognition, both regionally and nationally.

A retired public school teacher, she is now a member of the adjunct faculty of Drury College, Springfield, Missouri. Massey currently resides in Lebanon, Missouri, and actively promotes the appreciation of the Ozarks by speaking to regional groups.

I'm Calling To Say That Your Manuscript . . .

My abiding wish since college has been to write about rural family life. As I look back over the years, even though at times my activities were not deliberately directed toward this purpose, I realize now that every choice I've made and most happenings in my life have been preparing me toward reaching that goal. There were times when I couldn't write much because of other pressing duties, but there has never been a time that I haven't lived the rural life, gaining first-hand knowledge of my favorite subject.

Country people and living have always been my inspiration. I am from a farm background. My seven siblings and I still own the family farm in Vernon County, Missouri, where several generations of our family have lived. Although I was educated in Washington, D.C., where for many years my father worked, my family spent every summer on our farm. After college, I returned full time to live in rural southern Missouri.

My eastern teachers weren't interested in my writings about farm life, advising me to broaden my viewpoint, to experience something more. In the 1930s people were leaving the farms in droves for urban centers. America had grown up, become refined and cosmopolitan, no longer an agrarian society. Though many people had farm backgrounds, most, like my older brothers and sisters, wanted to get as far away from that life as possible. They had literally pulled themselves out of the mud and were on their way to more sophisticated life styles.

Since I've never been one to follow popular trends, I didn't share this escape from the farm. I didn't mind the more primitive living or the isolation from urban amenities, for I recognized values there that Americans were ignoring and therefore losing. Instead of broadening out into other circles, I wanted to deepen my experience of rural life in order to understand the strength of our pioneer past. That's what I wanted to write.

My teachers advised me to find a marketable subject. They pointed out that people read the *New Yorker*, or *Fortune*, or *Time*. No one wanted to read about life back on the farm.

I knew about city living. Since kindergarten, for nine months of the year I had lived in one of the most exciting cities in the nation. As the Washington representative of the American Farm Bureau, my father met presidents and was often with the senators and representatives on Capitol Hill. I saw important people, attended the theater and concerts, visited museums and art galleries, and used the Library of Congress. I even worked there for a few months and ate lunch in the cafeteria of the Supreme Court Building. However, I didn't want to write about that.

I read all the novels, essays, and poetry I could find about the westward movement and country life. Like Edwin Arlington Robinson's poem "Miniver Cheevy", I "loved the days of old" wishing that I had been born earlier so I could have ridden west in a wagon train and homesteaded some land. Since those experiences were not possible, my solution was to live in an area which still exhibited some of the pioneer characteristics. Ironically, what helped convince me was due to the efforts of my teachers who brought famous authors to my university. I heard in person Carl Sandburg and Robert Frost. Who could be more rural in subject matter than they?

Inspired by these great poets, and not convinced that mid-twentieth century writing had no room for rural subjects, after graduation I returned to Missouri. My first job was working among farm people as a home agent with the University of Missouri Agricultural Extension Service. I was sent to Laclede County in the central Missouri Ozarks where I have lived ever since.

I couldn't have found a more perfect setting. I relished the beautiful region which retained many of the traditional customs and values of post-pioneer living. I loved the people who accepted me immediately. In spite of my youth and inexperience, the older women politely listened to my demonstrations on how to can green beans in a pressure cooker, even though they had been canning them successfully for years. Since I had to drive over the hilly country roads, the men warned me to watch out for high water when crossing the many fords and low water bridges. After the first time someone frowned at my pronunciation, I learned to call the crossroad village of Orla, "Orly," because in the Ozarks an 'a' on the end of a word was given the long 'e' sound.

Knowing I would use the local speech in my writing, I jotted down the pronunciations, phrasing, and the colorful metaphors I heard. "She's so bowlegged she couldn't pen a pig in a ditch." Or "I'm so low I'd need a stepladder to kick a duck in the hiney." Although this was before the wide acceptance of using sexual terms in everyday speech, I was still amazed at the Victorian reluctance of some women to use words that had any sexual connotation. Though every farm owned one, the older woman wouldn't use the word "bull" because that would broadcast his sole purpose, which was to breed. He was the animal, the brute, or, my favorite, the gentleman cow. I was absorbing the speech along with everything else and gathering material to write.

One of the persons I met became my husband. We operated a stock farm on the Osage Fork River. Through him and his family, I became part of the community. For three or four years I was experiencing so much living that I didn't think too much about writing. I was encountering farming the old way, as Ozark farmers still used threshing machines and threw their hand-picked corn into a wagon drawn by mules.

Thinking back now to those farming years in relation to my writing, I consider them an apprenticeship. While delving deeper into Ozark living, I was also learning writing and marketing techniques. I wrote short articles for the local paper, or any publication that would print my work. I finished my first novel, a thinly disguised autobiography of my experiences on a farm.

I was so captivated by the region that I believed others would share my enthusiasm. Hopefully, I sent my manuscript to New York editors. I didn't know how to get a publisher or that I should meet other writers and writers' groups for feedback and advice. I wasn't even aware that there were magazines and books to help beginning writers. For years my novel went to many editors before I decided to give up on it and other manuscripts I was circulating also to no avail.

After the failure of my first big writing project to find a publisher, I didn't give up my wish to write. Realizing there would be no remuneration in writing, I accepted a teaching position in an isolated one-room school. Daily I drove the rocky roads over the hills and crossed the river on its low-water bridge. To reach the school during rainy weather I sometimes had to drive twenty-five miles out of the way to cross the river on a highway bridge. As I drove through low draws and fords in the road, water came up to the floor boards of my car. Wonderful experiences for stories.

Then events in my life crowded out temporarily my desire to write. My husband died suddenly. With a farm, a teaching position, and three young children, I had no time or energy to sit at my typewriter. My children and I continued on the farm for a few more years until moving to Lebanon, Missouri, where I taught English in the high school.

While teaching, I enjoyed vicarious pleasure from the writings of my students. Over the years I helped them produce their own publications – first a school newspaper, then a literary magazine, and finally *Bittersweet*. This was a professional quarterly about the Ozarks which developed a small but nationwide circulation. The students on the staff traveled all over the Ozarks to do research and interview older people.

I loved it! I was immersed in rural life, still learning more about the culture of the unique area in which the students and I lived. Since there was no market for their work, we created an outlet and developed a readership for the articles about places, people, and subjects of Ozark life.

Until I left Lebanon High School in 1986, the majority of my work with writing was as a teacher/advisor to my students' projects. They were the editors, writers, photographers, and artists, but since they were beginners, I helped them learn advanced writing techniques, such as how to organize vast amounts of material and how to catch and keep the reader's interest.

During this busy period I was itching to write myself but had time to do only some occasional articles for educational journals. The demands of my job and my own children left no time or energy for me to write. However, during those years I became a better writer as I learned along with my students. For instance, figuring out together how to organize the hours of transcribed taped material into an interesting, readable narrative helped me to improve the flow from one topic to another in my own manuscripts. Repeatedly pointing out to the students the value of interesting introductions and effective transitions throughout the articles has so ingrained those techniques into my writing that I automatically watch for weaknesses there as I do for spelling and grammar errors.

Any teacher of writing recognizes and points out these common faults to students. But there was a difference between my years of helping students improve their five hundred published articles from grading the papers of my regular class assignments. On my English students' papers, so that they would improve on the next composition, I merely put a grade with jotted brief comments, pointing out that the message could be enhanced by more sensory details or by tying the beginning and ending together. Marking these faults for the Bittersweet students meant they had to fix every problem. Together we had to figure out how to do that. They re-wrote many times until everyone on the staff was satisfied that the article was accurate and as professionally done as possible. Some students worked all semester on long, complicated topics. I didn't give them a grade. Their reward was publication.

The article was read, not just by the teacher, nor their peers at school, but by thousands of people from all over the United States and a few foreign countries. The student writers also knew that their articles would be in hundreds of libraries and available years later for scholarly research. Even during the ten years of *Bittersweet*'s publication, the quarterly was used as college texts and appeared in countless bibliographies. When selected articles from the magazine were published in book form, *Bittersweet Country* (1978 and 1986) and *Bittersweet Earth* (1985), the availability of the information became widespread.

With such readership, and because of their growing reputation of becoming experts on Ozark subjects, the students were determined to produce a professional product. We learned together. It was a wonderful work place for me, as well as the students, to improve our own skills in whatever field we chose to write.

My choice of subject matter has never changed. My work with the students only reinforced what I had already begun doing. They wrote about the Ozarks. They interviewed older men and women about many subjects. These self-sufficient people grew up in horse-and-buggy days in a beautiful, but basically poor area of rocks, hills, and trees. Making a living from the soil was difficult. Foremost in their accounts were the values of hard work, family, and Christian morals. And always they spoke with love of the land.

Often these Ozarkians lamented the passing of certain customs, such as neighborliness and strong marital and family commitments. They regretted the deterioration of some natural aspects such as the rivers filling up with gravel or the loss of the prairie grasses. But they lived in the present and were realistic about the past. The next words after telling us that we missed some special experience because we were not born yet were those agreeing that today also had advantages. "I wouldn't want to go back and do without electricity, for instance," one lady said. "I could, but I wouldn't want to."

What I have tried to do throughout my career is to encourage others to recognize and retain the best of the rural past. By teaching or through my writing, I try to bring out the values which I believe have made the United States the nation it is. Because of the isolated hill life, the older way of living has survived longer in the Ozarks than most other regions.

Rather than belittling this rural background or scorning the people as backward or inferior, we should recognize their knowledge, their ability to survive, their skills, and wit, and their stubborn independence. Using their ingenuity and know-how these people have made do with what they had, inventing substitutes for things they couldn't afford, and valuing relationships instead of possessions. These are admirable characteristics that should never go out of fashion.

I was able to continue publishing this type of literature for a time even after *Bittersweet* ceased publishing. In 1988 the Lebanon Publishing Company asked me to edit *Briarwood*, a new semi-annual, historical magazine about Laclede and surrounding counties. This was work from the staff of *The Lebanon Daily Record* and from free-lance writers. Though the subject matter was similar to that of *Bittersweet*, editing it was different from overseeing the students' work. The young people expected help and direction, willingly making changes and corrections. But I had to walk with velvet shoes around the full-grown egos of some of the professional writers to get the changes I wanted in their work, especially those trained in newspaper journalism. I wanted more detailed magazine articles, written in a more leisurely and personal style than the newspaper items and features they usually wrote.

This editing experience further honed my own writing skills and helped me better understand the publishing business. From professional writers and local people, who for the first time decided to send me their stories, I received some beautifully crafted articles from which I could learn; and I received some jumbled up ones that nonetheless contained a first-hand message no one else could write. I rejoiced on receiving the well-written ones. How much less time it took for me to put out an issue! No teaching, no rewrites. This editing business was great!

But the poorly done articles on topics I asked for and wanted to use presented a more difficult problem than I ever had with students. Sometimes the adult authors were happy to let me "fix" their problems. Other times it took diplomacy to suggest to them how they might enhance what they had written to fit our publication's needs and style. Most of the writers were people I'd known for years. I risked losing their friendship if I didn't handle them tactfully. But the alternative to making the needed improvements was to print a poor article. I wouldn't do that.

Since we didn't publish long enough to get more manuscripts than I could use, I wasn't rejecting the stories. I just wanted the writers to improve them. I understood their position because I had been on the receiving end of editors for years. Even now, after scores of rejections, I am still so pleased that an editor is interested in my work that I am willing to make the changes asked. Editing *Briarwood* helped me better understand the editor's reasons.

I was developing a group of reliable writers who were learning what I wanted. Each manuscript I received from them required less work for me to get it in print. Since *Bittersweet* had paved the way, we all believed that the local reading public was ready for this publication. However, after two years, we encountered the same problem that stopped *Bittersweet*. The small core of dedicated readers was not enough to support the magazines.

With greater understanding of editors and the publishing business, I left the field of periodicals and devoted myself to my own writing. I tried several types to find some medium editors might want. I wrote a musical drama based on Ozark themes. It was almost produced, but was canceled the day of the first rehearsal. I am still investigating markets for it.

At the instigation of some friends, I agreed to write a

biography of a remarkable Ozark woman, Mary Elizabeth Mahnkey from Taney County. She was a poet and a long-time rural correspondent. Research into her life presented a broad look at Ozark living from post-Civil War days to her death in 1948. I couldn't write about her without bringing in the Ozarks she lived in because that was what she also wrote about.

I had found someone else who loved the area and its people. She wrote beautifully, recording sayings, customs, and life as she lived it as she remembered it from her youth and her parents' stories. I was certain that this manuscript would easily find a publisher. But before they rejected it, two university presses were interested enough to begin editing. Believing in the manuscript, more to let the world know about Mrs. Mahnkey than getting one of my books published, I submitted it many times – even more than my first unpublished novel. Finally, after ten years and thirty-seven submissions, it was accepted by the University of Central Arkansas Press.

Since magazines, plays, and biographies weren't popular, I tried a different type of literature. As my first love was fiction, and I had learned much about writing and the market since I submitted my first novel, I returned to fiction. I wrote short stories and several novels. Naturally, all of the settings were in Missouri, mostly in the Ozarks, but also in my home area in western Missouri and my grandparents' home in north Missouri. All of the stories involve the rural area – strong family ties, good moral values, and love of the land.

A few of my short stories were published. Recently I finally found a publisher for some of my novels. I became acquainted with the editor of Avalon Books. Though romance novels were something I hadn't considered, I decided to try. Avalon's family-oriented books require strong moral values with no explicit love scenes and no swear words. The main problem was that the plots require a contemporary setting. At first that stopped me until I realized that I could put modern characters in situations where they needed to search the past to solve the problem.

In one book the legacy of a great-aunt caused the protagonist to research the history of her farm and discover the truth of an old legend. A hundred-year-old grave of an unknown woman killed on the railroad right-of-way caused a widow and her twin sons to delve into the past to find out the woman's story. I found that I could use my favorite setting and people in the action of the novels. While doing that, I was reaching a library audience far beyond the Ozarks.

My characters float the Ozark streams. They fall into sinkholes and explore caves. They operate huge combines on fields of wheat, and encased in a modern tractor, prepare the ground for corn planting. They raise goats and ride a Missouri Fox Trotting two-year-old horse to a world championship at Ava, Missouri. As they do these activities that are tied in with the plot of the story, the readers learn the values and customs of the people and the fragility of the land.

I know that two of the reasons it has taken me several decades to get published were my own writing inexperience and being side-tracked by other obligations. But perhaps a major reason was that when I started, the market for Ozark material was almost non-existent.

One purpose for starting *Bittersweet* was the lack of literature about the Ozarks. In 1970 I instigated a high school course about the Ozarks. I found very few books that I could use with my students. The main ones were Vance Randolph's books on folklore and Harold Bell Wright's novel, *The Shepherd of the Hills* based in Taney County, Missouri, and *The Calling of Dan Matthews* based in Lebanon, Missouri. Much of the literature I did find was making fun of the people or patronizing them. That I wouldn't use. So to help fill that void, my students published *Bittersweet* to present the true picture of the area.

Today, as we are moving still farther away from an agricultural society, and as the pockets of self-sufficient, rural living, like the Ozarks, disappear, those modes of living are historical rather than simply out-moded or backward. The people who left the farms now look back with nostalgia.

Evidence of that feeling is the booming tourist business in all parts of the Missouri and Arkansas Ozarks. Squeezed between the fun and the stereotyped hillbilly image they still find in theme parks and music shows, visitors are beginning to see something fundamental and solid.

In the more than twenty years since we started *Bittersweet*, there have been hundreds of poems, articles, stories, and books, both scholarly and popular, published about the Ozarks. Regional magazines like the *Ozarks Mountaineer* are flourishing. There are fine regional publishing houses, such as Seven Oaks Publishing Company, that are publishing serious and worthwhile material. This is a quite recent phenomenon.

My teachers in college who said no one would want to read about rural affairs were right for that time, but were wrong in the long run. My problem in school and with my first novel was that I was too soon. A few years later there was some interest in Missouri rural life. Even though there was enough support to initiate and sustain *Bittersweet* for ten years, my students' magazine didn't have the support in 1973-1983 that it would have now. I believe that if we were publishing now with more national interest in the region, we could garner a large enough subscription base that it could support itself.

One personal example of this change in the reading public is that now I have been able to publish in the *Ozarks*

Mountaineer portions of my first novel that had long been gathering dust. Since the stories were thinly fictional, all I had to do was to insert the real names of the people and places. The experiences I told were true, such as the shivaree the neighbors gave my husband and me a few days after we were married, my learning how to raise chickens and ducks, and my helping cook dinner for a huge siloing crew.

These pieces are now history, when at the time I tried to find a publisher, the events were still happening in my rural area. The New York based editors then had no interest in a backward culture in a hillbilly region. Now that some publishers have looked west of the Hudson River, and there are many fine publishing houses and periodicals in the center of the country and in the Ozarks itself, vignettes about country life are acceptable. I suppose the moral is to not give up. I hope that I live long enough to see this subject avidly sought after!

As the popularity of the Ozarks grows, so will the literature about the region. We have many talented writers who are busy at work as the reading public, editors, and publishers are becoming interested.

More optimistic of success now than at any time since writing my first manuscript, I'd like to branch into historical fiction. The Ozarks of Missouri and Arkansas have hundreds of stories that need to be told – stories that few people know about. Who, for instance, outside a few local Civil War buffs, knows about Order No. 11? In western Missouri during the Civil War over 20,000 people were moved out of four counties on the Kansas border, their property confiscated or burned with no restitution. To me that is a prime setting for a novel.

Even the people who have lived in the Ozarks all their lives, don't know much about their history. I try to fill that gap in my talks and my graduate education classes at Drury

College in Springfield. Most of my students are from the area. At the end of the course one student wrote:

> Studying American history I came to realize the repetitiveness of the information provided. It was the same story about the Pilgrims and then the Revolutionary War's battles. I received a very limited picture of America in the 1800s. I feel that I missed out on a very important part of my heritage. I was not told about the segregated cultures that formed across Missouri and how the area's conditions allowed for preservation and emergence of customs, music, and other art forms. To understand Ozark culture is to realize that this area is not inhabited by a bunch of 'dumb hillbillies.' It is an area that puts a value on preserving the family and culture.

If local people learn very little about their area, how much more is the ignorance of outsiders, even about the physical aspects of the region that they see when they visit. In my Elderhostel classes at the YMCA of the Ozarks at Potosi, Missouri, I teach educated and professional people from all over the United States. Though they know next to nothing about the Ozarks when they first arrive, as the class progresses, they become fascinated. They continually tell me of their prior misconceptions and ignorance. In my week-long class on Ozark culture, I try to cover a little bit of everything – geology, history, customs, and folklore. Once when I was explaining the karst topography of the Ozark Plateau, I was insecure because one of the men in the class was a Ph.D. in geology. Afterwards I told him he should have explained the geological formations. "Oh, no," he quickly assured me, "I know nothing about geology of the Ozarks."

I was appalled. This 50,000 square mile formation in the middle of the country that is larger than most eastern states is geologically different from anything around it. Yet an expert in the science knew nothing of it!

I shouldn't have been surprised. I've seen evidence again and again that outsiders really do not know the true Ozarks. To further illustrate the lack of information about the area, until recent years there has been very little serious, academic study about its pre-historic inhabitants. In history books, as my graduate student wrote, the role of Missouri and Arkansas in the Civil War is rarely told, even though Missouri was vital to both sides. The war actually started on the Missouri-Kansas border seven years before Fort Sumter, and the people who tried to live in the Ozarks probably suffered more and longer than even those in occupied southern states. This and much more is prime material that needs to be written.

Happily, the situation is reversing. There is more academic study about the region and its people, and there are many good articles and books being published. I have been told that part of the impetus for the now expanding market for Ozark material is because of the students' work on *Bittersweet*. Though I doubt that we had any major effect, I am pleased. The truth is more that we just happened to do our work at the time the public was becoming aware of its own heritage and contributions. As we approach the twenty-first century, we in mid-America realize that we have a history right here. We do not depend on the East or Europe for all of our historical information and cultural background.

I am excited about the possibilities. We have untold stories in Ozark settings, our writers have the talent, and the outlets for our work are increasing. Though it took me many years to prove it, I was right about the value of writing about our rural heritage. As our fund of literature builds up, perhaps in a few years the literary world will recognize the Ozark writers as a group as it does the New England authors of the last century, those of the Irish Renaissance, or writers of the

New South. It is about time. And I'd be proud when that recognition comes if I'm one of the writers on the list.

Until then, I'll continue writing and submitting manuscripts about my favorite people and region in hopes that some editor will telephone me saying, "I'm calling to say that your manuscript has been accepted . . ."

Velda Brotherton

Velda Brotherton is the city editor and feature writer for a small weekly newspaper in Washington County, Arkansas. She has published numerous articles and been published in national publications such as *Country America*.

Her first book, *Wandering in the Shadows of Time: An Ozarks Odyssey*, was published by Seven Oaks Publishing Company. Under her pseudonym Elizabeth Gregg, she has written two historical romance novels for Topaz-Penguin USA, and has recently signed a contract for two more. Her latest book, *Moonspun Dreams*, was released in August 1995.

She is active in several writers organizations and is a member of the Ozark Writers League board of directors.

Brotherton was born in a log cabin near Shepherd Springs, Arkansas, and currently lives on a mountain near Winslow, Arkansas.

Saleable Articles Begin With A Great Interview

There's no magic or set rule for conducting those special interviews that will result in the kind of article that will mean an immediate sale. But one thing is for sure. You'd better genuinely like people and care about them, their lives, their hopes and dreams, and most of all their precious memories.

Now, once that is settled, it's time to get to work. I learned some special tricks as I conducted interviews, you can too.

First, you have to schedule your interviews. Opportunities for that most perfect of interviews can come from just about anywhere. Rarely will anyone realize the gold mine they are offering you – It's up to you to see for yourself.

One interview I will never forget came about when I received a telephone call inviting me to Retta Neville's ninetieth birthday party at her church. This was a good enough piece for the weekly local newspaper for which I write features, but not good enough for my interview. I asked if there was a chance I could interview her elsewhere. My caller casually mentioned that Retta lived in the home her father built when the family came to Arkansas in 1884. My gold mine! No question about it, I wanted to speak with this lady in her home with all her memories, ghosts, if you will, surrounding her. Together we could step back into the past, and I knew that was the ideal place in which to do it. As it turned out, of course it was. I met ghosts I never would have met in a crowded church at a birthday party.

Who could resist this tale?

> "When we would gather it always meant music. Uncles would come from Oklahoma and bring their banjos, two of my brothers played the violin, and we girls would sing till we couldn't sing no more."
>
> "We had party lines, you know, and these old crank phones. When we'd have musicals we'd turn the crank and everyone would pick up and leave their phone off the hook so they could listen."

I never expected such a story, and it came about because we were speaking about an old piano in the shadowy corner of the main room of her "home place."

Later many of her relatives were astonished that Retta had told me so many stories. A cousin remarked, "But she's almost deaf, how did you get her to understand your questions?"

Questions? I'm not sure I remember forming any definite questions with my voice. I do know that I lay my hand on hers, felt the warm blood pulsing through the fine veins just beneath her crepe-paper skin; I looked into her eyes and I spoke of the world of memories in which I was sure she spent most of her time. And so she put those memories into words for me. Words I recorded for keepsakes.

Not only did I get the story of the crank telephones, but I got something else. I felt her emotions and heard what she heard: the plucking of strings, the clear tones of childish voices raised in song, the rhythmic thunk of shabby work boots on the pine board floors under my own feet as I sat beside this elderly woman. She rocked and nodded her head, tapped her palms on the wooden arms of her chair, and brought to life the most wondrous visions. For a long while after I left that old log cabin in the wilderness, I felt as if I had literally taken a trip backward in time.

Consider this:

> "Times were hard in those days. One time we were down to our last silver dollar. Every day Logan would go looking for work and he'd take that silver dollar with him. When he'd come home he'd grin and show it to me, tell me he hadn't needed it that day. What he didn't say was that he had walked everywhere he went and gone without a noon meal. We had that silver dollar until sometime after we moved onto this place in 1955. But then someone stole it."
>
> She looked at me for a long beat, her eyes glistening with a staunch pride. In that moment I sensed that she had shared with me much more about their lives than the theft of one silver dollar.

This quote came about at the end of an interview. I had spent a long while with the couple because they were childhood friends of my mother's, and so would have been hurt if I had cut my visit short. This woman had not spoken much during my long and extremely fruitful interview with her husband, the self-appointed storyteller of the clan. But her tale of the silver dollar is exactly the kind of hidden jewel I look for. Here I had uncovered unexpected insight into their lives.

Both of these interviews and the quotes are included in my book, *Wandering in the Shadows of Time: An Ozarks Odyssey*, published by Seven Oaks Publishing Company in 1994.

To write articles and books from interviews requires much more than does reporting news stories. Who, what, where, when, why, and how are all important, but they skim only the surface. Answers to those questions are not nearly enough to flesh out the real story, the one the reader of features wants to know.

When I go out on an interview, I already know something about my subject, most importantly why I want to interview him in the first place. Most of my interviews originated because I wanted to do a feature for the weekly newspaper for which I write. It never occurred to me at the time that I would one day be turning the best of those interviews into a book. I'm glad I kept very good notes, and in some cases tapes, but beyond that I kept a memory file. For as I went about doing my job, my emotions were in play. I was conscious of what went on around me when I couldn't take notes. Everyone reacts to situations differently, depending on their background. Only I (only you) can write the stories I (you) write, and they will not be like any others.

Everything I've ever known, seen and done, comes into play and that is what I add to make an article or book uniquely mine as no one else could write it. It's how things make me feel that count:

> Dancing pollen laces the air where sunlight breaks through the canopy of leaves that close in on me as I go higher and higher up the mountain . . . As I start to leave huge snowflakes drift lazily down through the trees. There's a stillness so total as to be unreal. It's a silence so deep that I can hear the puffs of snow light on my skin.

Again, quotes from my book, examples of what I remembered, more than what I wrote down or taped. They go past interviews and make the world real to the reader.

It's so important to be aware of your surroundings, not just the subject of the interview. See what he sees, feel what he feels, remember what he remembers, and then when you write the piece add the crowning touch. Show your personal and emotional reaction that went beyond the words he spoke. Once you can learn not to be afraid to do that, you will turn the corner and go from a competent writer to an excellent writer.

When conducting an interview, remember, communication is not only talking, it is listening. Learning to do so without interrupting to put in your own "two cents worth" is an art worth cultivating. Always resist telling stories unless it is necessary to break the ice and convince a subject to recount some tales of his own. I let the interview go where it will, let it wander a bit from the questions I've prepared. Many times this method has uncovered exciting and unexpected tales. Control of your subject may be important when interviewing for a news story, but there are far more considerations for feature stories. I'm looking for the unforeseen tale, the unusual or hidden memory that will make my piece stand out.

A man is more than his name and what he does. He is the substance of his family, of their beliefs, his past, his hopes and dreams. To uncover these things a good interviewer has to adopt a tell-me-a-story-attitude. Beg him to amaze, shock, make you laugh and cry. And most important, don't be ashamed to cry with him as you would laugh with him. I often do.

Once the interview is finished, the goal is to tell a riveting story, not report an incident. This is especially true when turning interviews into articles or a book. A reader does not pick up this kind of piece to learn facts and figures, he is looking for insight into human nature, he is looking to relate to other beings of his kind, he wants to know he is not alone in his own personal joys and sorrows. But most of all he wants to be entertained by a story.

Conducting interviews, I believe, can only be truly and well learned by doing. As I mentioned before, you'd better genuinely like people or this type of writing isn't for you.

There are other rules too, the most obvious being never ask a question if the answer can be yes, no, okay or maybe. Rephrase these kinds of questions. Not, "Did you attend a one-room school?" but, "Is it true that when you went to a one-room school they hung quilts over the windows to keep out the cold?" Chances are, the subject will go you one better and tell you something else unusual. It's a way of making conversations, and it works much better than questions and answers. This style of interviewing also puts the subject at ease. Don't push. Sometimes it's not so bad to just sit together and stare out over the fields in silence for a few minutes. If you're attentive and relaxed you'll get a good interview.

Because a subject and I sat companionably on his front porch and stared in silence across the rutted road that led from his home into the Ozark National Forest and an utter wilderness, I got this wonderful quote.

> "I'm afraid they're gonna try to get the water line through here and condemn all our wells. The Forestry has already come and put back all those varmints on us and tell us we can't kill rattlesnakes. Never knew a hillbilly to let a rattlesnake get away. Years ago we could hear the panthers squalling of a morning, but we don't hear 'em anymore. Reckon they all fell out of the trees, dead."

All spoken without my ever asking a question.

One thing I've learned, when doing interviews with

old timers, especially in the Ozarks: never get in a hurry.

There's something to be said about knowing when an interview is over, though. As important as not going away too soon, is don't overstay your welcome. Watch for signs that you've stayed long enough. Many of my interviews are conducted with elderly folks. I can always go back for another visit, in fact almost all of them ask me to return when I do leave. Polite hill folks always ask you to "stay more." Learn to know when they mean it and when they wish you'd just turn tail and skedaddle.

Finding people to interview may seem tough at first, but it gets easier. I obtain interviews in many ways. Working for a newspaper does have its advantages, because my readers all know what I do and are eager to supply me with subjects. Many times their idea of a good interview and mine don't coalesce, but those precious times they do are invaluable.

However, there are other ways to find good subjects if you don't work in the "public eye." Tell people what you are doing. Your friends and relatives, merchants in your hometown, the librarian, a reporter friend, anyone. Check news items in local newspapers for unusual ideas. A reporter may write a news piece about something that you can turn into a feature with an entirely different slant once you have interviewed the subject yourself. Not every lead you get will work out, but many will.

It's important as well, to know where to conduct an interview. Because of the style of my writing, I like to interview folks on their home territory and face to face rather than by telephone. If I do use a tape recorder, which I don't always, I also take notes. Too many distracting sounds can ruin a tape or make some of it unintelligible. Besides, it is quicker to decipher notes and come up with a good piece. A perfect quote or two can then be picked up by listening to the tape. When writing on a deadline this method is valuable.

But most important of all, and I can't stress this too much: Keep your inner ear, your sixth sense if you will, on the alert. The spirit of a life well lived has resonance, it pulses around us, but we have to be open to it. I experienced a very poignant moment following an interview with a man whose great-grandfather had fought on the "wrong" side in the Civil War, thus causing a rift that never healed in generations of his family. As I left the company of this man who had related this tragic story, I could have sworn I saw a young man in a tattered gray uniform standing in the deep shadows of a sycamore tree a short way down the creek, watching us. That vision, hallucination, illusion, whatever it might have been, remained with me and made its way into the book, though not the piece I wrote for the paper.

Many times one interview will lead to yet another. During several visits I had with folks in one area over a period of a few months, people kept making casual remarks about the post office that ran away, laughing and joking, but not able to tell me the whole story. In an unrelated, wonderful interview with a barber still cutting hair at the age of ninety-one, I finally got a lead on who could tell me the story of the post office. Both the barber's wonderful tale about pitching Indian Head Pennies and the story of the runaway post office made the newspaper feature page and are included in my book.

That's why I always file away in my memory and my notes odd little pieces of information that may have absolutely nothing to do with the feature I'm working on. One day that notation will be fodder for an entirely different tale.

It's difficult to say what works best when writing a piece from any particular interview. I usually fall down right in the middle and write away, going back later to add and detract and work up a good lead. In that way my initial impressions tend to come out the tips of my fingers without too much coaxing. We can sometimes think too much and ruin the spontaneity of our writing. As to the way to tell your tale, it differs depending on your feel for the piece, the rhythm and sense you wish to convey. For my book I choose to utilize an unusual style of tense and first and third person because I wanted the reader to feel as if he were wandering with me during all my travels and interviews, as if everything were just at that moment happening.

I decided not to put my questions in dialogue and wrote myself into each piece in first person, present tense, letting the subjects tell their stories in the past tense. While a bit more difficult to do, the style gave the book the rhythm and sense of being that I wanted. This also allowed me to be "present" and voice my own memories and thoughts to the reader only.

There are many ways to approach the writing of a good interview so it will become a saleable piece. Much of that can depend on the market, of course. We cannot put ourselves in newspaper features, except in rare cases. Modern journalism tends to lean more in that direction, but for the most part, the editorial *we* still stands and even *we* don't voice opinions and asides or tell how we feel about something, unless we are writing an editorial for the opinion page.

Some magazines might like the approach I took, but it would be wise to know your market and then outline the style you wish to use in your query. That is precisely what I did for the book.

In fiction, there is much talk about the writer's "voice." I believe we all have a voice that we use in all of our writing. Sometimes, when it is necessary, we quell that voice and write for the market. Nothing is so wonderful as to be able to write in our own natural voice and be able to sell what we write. I have been fortunate, but it did not happen overnight. It took years of hard work and the very stubborn idea that I was good enough to one day succeed.

All I can suggest to the novice writer is to network, attend conferences, join a writer's group and learn your craft. Then, when you're sure you know the craft, learn some more. This is true whether you are writing articles, short stories or long fiction. The cream comes to the top is an old cliche, but the truth of a saying is what makes it a cliche. The first step for you is to add your cream to the milk, so to speak. Over and over and over.

My career came along late in life, I was fifty by the time I had written my first novel. After years of diligent work, I sold two books, a non-fiction and a fiction, in the few months prior to my fifty-eighth birthday. Both were sold through contacts I made at writer's conferences.

Some tell me that almost nine years is not very long to wait, but the secret is, I didn't wait. I got out there and went to work in the field, and had written nine books, and numerous articles and short stories by the time I published.

Because I am an ordinary person with no specific training in writing, either formal or otherwise, my success might be viewed as a fluke, sort of like winning a lottery. But I had a desire to write, discovered I had a talent for it, but didn't settle for that. I honed and polished and then when I was ready, faced the publishing world with what I had to offer. And there is much more where that came from.

Whether you are twenty, thirty, or eighty, a dream is worth pursuing. Never give it up because you think you are too old. You have to travel the path anyway, so why not enjoy all it offers? What's important is that you did what you wanted to do along the way. I am very pleased to be leaving words behind for the enjoyment of my children and grandchildren and perhaps a few other readers who run across my books along the way.

Photo: Robert Poole

Max McCoy

Max McCoy is an award-winning author and journalist. A native of Baxter Springs, Kansas – at the edge of the Ozark Plateau – his stories are often drawn from regional and historical themes.

His first novel, *The Sixth Rider*, was based on the 1892 raid on Coffeyville, Kansas, by the Dalton Gang. It won the Medicine Pipe Bearer's Award in 1991 for the best first novel from the Western Writers of America.

McCoy is currently writing the *Indiana Jones* series of original novels for Bantam/Lucasfilm. The latest book in the series, *Indiana Jones and the Philosopher's Stone*, was released in May 1995.

He currently lives in Pittsburg, Kansas, and his hobbies include scuba diving, black powder weapons, and classic Mustangs.

The happy ending of the fairy tale,
the myth, and the divine comedy of
the soul, is to be read, not as a
contradiction, but as a transcendence
of the universal tragedy of man.

– Joseph Campbell
The Hero With a Thousand Faces

Most Of What Follows Is True:
Writing Today's Western

Having been asked to contribute a chapter on The Writing of the Western, and despite having written a few modest examples of the category, I am faced with a nagging problem: I don't know what a western really *is*.

And if you think *you* do, you're wrong.

The western is changing too fast for the old stereotypes to hold true. Gone are the days of the cereal company horse opera, and you can no longer tell the good guys from the bad guys just by the color of their hats. The guys now are just as likely to be gals, and a lot of westerns aren't even set in the west anymore, at least not in the geographic or temporal sense. The west has become a state of mind, rather than a direction or a period.

But then, it always was.

I'm going to share with you how I go about writing books that are marketed as westerns, but it is certainly not the only way. And I don't always do it the same way twice. If some of the techniques that I use work for you, fine. You're welcome to them.

Just remember that nobody can teach you how to write, and that you need to take all advice about writing with more than just a grain of salt. If somebody claims to be able to teach you how to write, then you had better run like hell, because all they want is your money.

What others *can* teach you is proper manuscript form, how to sharpen your material, how to market that material, and what it is (for now) that editors think they are looking for. But none of this is brain surgery. There really are no rules. There are as many paths to publication as there are writers. The important thing is to keep learning, keep writing, and have fun.

Because if writing isn't fun – or satisfying, or rewarding, or whatever else you want to call it – then you had better find another dream and follow it. If you are in it for the money, then you had better find another scheme, because all of the writers I know that are making money (even the ones that I consider to be bad writers) started writing because they loved to tell a story. Some of them even gave up careers as doctors and lawyers and such to pursue careers as novelists, and one of my mentors – Don Coldsmith, a terrifically successful western writer – not only abandoned a medical career, but did it at an age when most folks are thinking of retiring. More about Don later, because he's the type of person you should try to emulate if you're serious about this business.

Writing is an intensely personal journey, one that nobody else can make for you. It is nothing less than the adventure described by Joseph Campbell as the *hero's journey*. Along the way, you will meet people who hinder you and some who help you, but your success will ultimately depend upon you alone. And if you are not independently wealthy, then you will have to figure out a way to feed yourself, and your kids if you have them, while you serve out your apprenticeship.

A fortune spent in reading fees will not make you a

writer. Neither will a college degree, a vanity press, a new computer, the latest edition of *Writer's Digest*, or a really cool addiction. There was a time when I thought that smoking a pipe would make me a writer – I guess I was fourteen or fifteen when I began – and now, a couple of decades later, it is proving damned hard to quit. But there are harder habits to break. Don't be encouraged by the legacy of Hemingway and Fitzgerald to take up drinking simply because it seems literary – both of their lives were cut short and neither seemed terribly happy.

The only habit that will make you a writer is writing. It takes hard work and dedication. A little talent never hurts, but that is not absolutely required – as the bestseller lists attest, some writers regularly make fortunes without it.

Writing is the most democratic profession in the world. It doesn't matter what you look like, or how old you are, or how many degrees you have (or don't have) after your name.

There seems to be a lot of confusion among aspiring authors surrounding this passage to Writerdom. Many seem to think that there is some kind of magic formula or secret handshake that will open the doors of New York publishing.

This attitude was summed up for me a couple of years ago while teaching a small group session at the Tallgrass Writing Workshop. The workshop is held on the campus of Emporia (Kansas) State University – where I used to teach before fearing that academia would suck out my very soul – and I had grown accustomed to the motion sensors on some of the light switches there. These devices shut off the lights when no motion is detected in the classroom after several minutes. One afternoon I was sitting on the edge of the desk with my arms folded, waxing philosophic to a workshop group – and the group was rather sluggish as well, having just come back from lunch – so the lights went out. Being used to this phenomenon, and without skipping a word, I waved my arms over my head and the lights returned. An astonished look came over a particularly charming older woman in the front row. "Why," she declared, "no wonder you're published. If you can do that, you can do anything."

Getting published is really not that mysterious.

I'm going to give you my two most valuable pieces of advice right here, up front, so you can think about them. They are too important to save for the end, and they are so simple that they tend to be overlooked. And they apply whether you write westerns or science fiction or mysteries.

Believe in Yourself.

Have Something to Say.

First, you must have a bullet-proof belief in yourself. This is necessary in order to sustain one through all the rejection that is a natural part of writing, not to mention life. I'm not talking here of a swaggering, aggressive kind of belief – that behavior will turn people off quicker than just about anything else – but cultivate instead a quiet, secure belief in yourself as a writer. Right now, begin to think of yourself as a *writer*.

Secondly, in order to write, you must have something to say. In other words, you must find something that is worth writing about. To do that, you must know yourself and know your subject. Find the one story you would most like to write in the world, the one that you are uniquely qualified to write, the one that you were meant to write. Something that brings you tears of joy or cries of pain – or preferably both – every time you think of it.

Your life thus far has been a journey that has prepared you to write this story. No one else is as qualified or has the necessary insight. There is an old adage in this profession that you're supposed to "write what you know." I would amend that to: Write about that which you feel passionately, that which you are willing to learn about, that which is significant to you. If the story is difficult to pin down, you must ask yourself this question: "What is it that makes me feel and think and bleed?"

Got it?

The rest is a piece of cake.

The American Monomyth

Are you with me so far?

Good, because a lot of people would have bailed simply because of the word "western" in the title. The category has become synonymous, for much of the book-buying public, with bad writing, shallow characterization, and formulaic stories. People who actually read westerns, of course, know better.

And if you run across a book that seems lacking, forgive the poor fool who wrote it – and we are all fools from time to time – and resolve that yours will be better. One of the most powerful motivations for a writer is to throw a book down in disgust and declare, "I could have done better than that!" If you feel that way, then back up your talk with action and *do it*.

Every couple of years or so a critic will declare that the western is dead. And every time, nothing could be farther from the truth. Because the western is uniquely American, going back perhaps as far as James Fenimore Cooper, and because it keeps evolving and showing up in new forms, it will never die. It has become a part of what we as Americans are and satisfies our universal need for a mythic hero. The cowboy is larger than life, and this is why the western is such an easy target for those who would dismiss it as the intellectual equivalent of chewing gum.

And that is a mistake.

The graceless age in which we live is sorely in need of heroes. Because we find such little spiritual sustenance in our everyday world, we turn to stories. And it is an old, old story that we want.

Joseph Campbell, the mythologist I mentioned earlier, called it the "monomyth." The word, if not its meaning, is from Joyce, and it refers to the ubiquitous hero adventure in human culture. The hero's journey, Campbell said, is recognizable in every culture in the world and in many religions.

"A hero ventures forth from the world of common day into a region of supernatural wonder," Campbell wrote. "Fabulous forces are there encountered and a decisive victory is won: the hero comes back from this mysterious adventure with the power to bestow boons on his fellow man."

The names and faces change, but the story remains the same. Not only are these stories important in passing along culture and helping society to pull together, Campbell said, but they also provide guidance for individual lives.

Campbell had a suspicion that for every psychological "block" a person experienced, there is an appropriate mythological story – a key narrative, if you will – that would help the individual overcome the blockage. And, he said, one way to go about finding this key narrative was perusing the works of a good novelist.

The western is the Americanized version of the monomyth. It is the same old story, but set in a different framework: the frontier is the magical realm where the hero must face his or her greatest challenge in order to revitalize society. Because of this underlying pattern, the reader brings a particular set of expectations to the western (and any other story that is based on the hero's journey).

Although the unchanging monomyth provides the structure for the western, the details of story and characterization are constantly changing to keep pace with our society. This has brought changes in the western which has lifted it from the "horse opera" days of forty years ago to a currently sophisticated level of storytelling.

My friend Don Coldsmith teaches a course on westerns at Emporia State University, and he is in a better position to know about such things than your average academic. Not only is he a successful western author, with thirty or more books to his credit, but when he lectures – and writes – he knows what he's talking about. In addition to his novelizing, he maintains a small cattle operation. He has changed careers several times in his life, and at various items has been a muleskinner, an gunsmith, a taxidermist, a Congregational preacher, and most recently, a family physician. Muleskinners, by the way, don't skin the animals, they drive them. I'm not sure what exactly a Congregational preacher does, but it sounds uplifting.

The traditional Western, Don says, has six identifiable characteristics, ranging from time period to the reputation of the genre. Don's list, along with my interpretations, follows. And so there will be no mistake, this is the type of western that you *don't* have to write to become published:

◆ Set in a thirty-five year period, from the end of the Civil War to 1900. This roughly corresponds to the zenith of the American cowboy, whose numbers were never great, but whose influence on American culture remains enormous.

◆ Located west of the Mississippi River. Although the American frontier has marched steadily westward, the frontier was firmly west of the Great River after the Civil War. By the turn of the century, the continent was regarded as settled – the frontier had vanished.

◆ The characters tend to be two-dimensional. Cowboy heroes are strong, silent types whose actions speak louder than words. The strongest clue to characterization may be the color of a character's clothing.

◆ No overt sex. The cowboy is more likely to kiss his horse than to kiss the girl, Don says. Also, I would add, cowboys are always heterosexual.

◆ Women and minorities are seldom portrayed as strong characters. More often than not, women are viewed as helpless without men. Indians are less than human. Cowboys are almost exclusively white, although the historical record indicates that at least one in five were black or Mexican. And seldom, even for a moment, does the point-of-view shift to a minority.

◆ The genre is held in low regard by scholars. Historical authenticity is questionable. Research was not regarded as essential for a successful western.

An example of the traditional western is *Hondo*, by Louis L'Amour, published in 1953. Although it does not have all the characteristics listed here – L'Amour, for example, was noted for his authenticity – it has enough to be considered traditional.

The new western, in contrast, isn't bound to any of these rules. Some stories don't even take place in the West – or even America. Women and minorities (especially Indians) are often the protagonists, and sex is treated in a much more realistic manner. In fact, there's even a couple of "adult" western series. And, Don says, there is a growing acceptance of the Western in college literature classes.

The west is not a direction, but a state of mind. It is the frontier, any frontier, during any documented time period. The contemporary Australian outback, for example. Or the American colonies prior to 1776. Or Kansas at the time the first Europeans saw it. The frontier is nothing less that Campbell's "region of supernatural wonder."

A good example of a new western, I think, is Coldsmith's *Spanish Bit Saga*. It begins in 1542, when a band of plains Indians adopts a young Spanish conquistador who has become separated from Coronado's expedition. The soldier never rejoins his own people, but passes a series of trials to eventually become a leader of his adopted tribe. Subsequent books follow the descendants of Juan Garcia and the tribe. It is no coincidence that the most avid fans of this series are hooked by the spiritual aspects of the story.

Which is the monomyth at work.

Don, by the way, has often told me that he feels the spaghetti westerns popular during the 1970s were ultimately failures because there were no good guys and bad guys, only bad guys and worse guys. Now, I don't know if I fully agree with him – the title of the most popular of these films was *The Good, the Bad, and the Ugly* – but he does have a point. The difference, I suppose, is how you define "good." And in the 1960s, as I remember, good was defined as just about anything which questioned authority.

Since I tend to be fascinated by things which threaten the status quo (I was a notorious troublemaker in school), I am naturally inclined to take up for the spaghetti epics. I guess that's why I find myself writing about outlaws and other misfits. Society must constantly reinvent itself in order to survive, so consequently it finds itself in a symbiotic – and ironic – relationship with these rebels. That's why, I think, so many heroes are portrayed as outcasts in the beginning. Don, by the way, prefers the term "free thinker" rather than outcast. But then, Don grew up in an age when good was defined (usually) as that which obeyed authority.

Because Don's expectations were dashed by Clint Eastwood's no-name hero, these films – for him and many others like him – are not satisfying westerns. They fail to transcend the universal tragedy.

Any short list of new westerns would have to include works by writers such as Judy Alter, Fred Bean, Win Blevins,

Max Evans, and Michael and Kathleen O'Neal Gear. All of them successfully incorporate features of the new western into their work.

A final word on the "new" western: it isn't really new. People have been writing them, on and off, for some time. But in the past, the book-buying public wasn't quite ready for them, with the exception of two wonderful novels published in the 1960s: *True Grit*, by Charles Portis, and *Little Big Man*, by Thomas Berger.

Story

Story encompasses all of the what-happens and what-ifs in the novel. Some people call this plot, although I think that is too narrow a definition. "Story" is broader, and really more useful, because it includes such things as structure and narrative. Is it told in the first person or third person? What's the idea or premise? Is there a historical hook to the novel? Is there a satisfying ending?

Characterization is considered by many editors to be the more important of the two. Compelling characters, they say, will often carry a weak story. And it is the synthesis of story and characterization that makes a successful novel.

I'm constantly amazed that the question I'm most often asked about my writing is, "Where do you get your ideas?" The answer: everywhere. The world is bursting with ideas. The question is not how do you get an idea for a book, but how you choose the right idea from a myriad of possibilities.

I frequently (but not always) jot down the book ideas that occur to me, and they come from many different sources: a bit of conversation overheard at the local cafe, a visit to a museum, the name of a town on a very old map. More often than not, the ideas come from what I call "The Gray Line" –

the murky division between conventional knowledge and the vast unknown. This is the domain of myth and mysticism, legend and conjecture.

But how do you know when you have the right story?

That is something only your gut can tell you. Lukewarm ideas need not apply – you won't be able to sustain interest over two or three hundred manuscript pages. If a writer finds a story tedious, then what chance does the reader have? But if the story is so compelling that you can hardly wait to get writing, if the characters seem as real to you as your closest friends, and if you are convinced that you have some special insight or divine guidance that will make you tell the story better than anyone else could, then go with it. Now is the time to write those sample chapters and that synopsis, while the material is still fresh. Hard work is important, but there really is no substitute for enthusiasm.

Writers are active, indefatigable seekers of knowledge. They ask questions. They check facts. And inevitably, they think for themselves. Many books – including my award-winning first novel, *The Sixth Rider* – began with a simple "What if ?"

What if, I asked, the legendary sixth rider who escaped the destruction of the Dalton Gang following the bloody raid on Coffeyville's banks in 1892 was a teen-aged Dalton brother? I had run across the story of the sixth rider during my newspaper days, when I did an article on the Dalton Defenders museum in Coffeyville. Six bandits were seen riding into town the day of the raid, but when the gunsmoke had cleared, only five outlaws – four of them dead and one critically wounded – were accounted for. The mystery intrigued me. What if one told the story in the first person, from the youngest brother's point of view? How would it feel to ride with the infamous Dalton Gang, to rob banks and trains and to become a folk hero while thumbing your nose at law? And how would it feel when the reality finally hit home that this was serious, deadly business?

There are literally millions of "what ifs" out there, waiting to be explored in fiction. The difference between a novelist and a wannabe is how one handles those ideas. It's not enough just to have the idea, but you have to get it down on paper. And to get it down effectively takes work.

Many writers, including myself, adopt a familiar pattern or structure for their stories once they have chosen the basic idea or premise. The Hero's Journey provides an excellent pattern. So does Greek mythology, the Arthurian legends, even poetry – I've often considered recasting Beowulf as a western. Just when the hero thinks he's met his biggest challenge by gunning down the villain, look out, because here comes Ma and is she ever upset! Another tactic is to structure your novel after somebody else's novel – this really isn't stealing, after all, since you're still telling the story in your own way.

Once you know the story you're going to tell, a good way to begin is to start in the middle or near the end. Place your characters in a desperate situation, one in which the conflict and consequences are immediately apparent, and see what happens. There's no need to begin with what your characters had for breakfast that morning or even to give an account of why the Dalton boys rob banks and trains. Show them in action, and there will be plenty of time to explain their reasons later. The more compelling you can make your opening, the more likely a reader is to pull your book off the shelf and take it home.

That's the kind of opening I tried for in *The Sixth Rider*.

Characterization

Characterization is the art of conveying personality through description. This can be accomplished with wonderful economy by a revealing remark, gesture, or habit. Just as in real life, the clothes your characters wear, their manner of speech, and especially their actions, are clues to what kind of individuals they are.

But don't make them *too* consistent. To be compelling, a character must be complex. Even the most despicable of villains should have a glimmer of compassion. Make it even more difficult for your hero. Give him or her one fatal flaw – it could be alcoholism, bigotry, anything – that threatens to undo all of the good work your hero has accomplished so far.

Actions speak louder than words. Avoid the tendency to have your characters describe their every emotion, and rationalize their every action, through dialogue. Also avoid trying to help the reader along by telling them outright what your characters are feeling.

Instead, *show* the reader.

If you have a character who has just lost a child, don't tell the reader she was sad. Show the tears running down her cheeks and her fists clenched so tightly that her nails are cut into her palms. Make the reader share the empty feeling in the pit of her stomach and taste the vomit that rises in her throat.

Showing instead of telling is much more convincing. There are times, of course, when exposition is necessary, but try to keep this to a minimum. Stick to the story, and write cinematically – think of the story as a series of scenes that unfold in the reader's mind. This contributes to what Samuel Taylor Coleridge called the "willing suspension of disbelief." This happens when one is so caught up in the story that you forget that it's *just* a story.

Sometimes, it's easier to model characters after people you know. This can backfire, however, when your subject recognizes him- or herself and decides that it is a rather unflattering portrayal. As a rule, if you have a character who is clearly drawn from life, it is better to stick with people who are public figures – politicians, actors, and so forth.

If you stick with writing fiction, you will eventually discover that some characters have a life of their own. What they do may surprise you. Don't let this bother you, however, because your subconscious probably has a reason for it. It also adds an element of realism, because people *are* unpredictable. And instead of hopelessly skewering characterization by introducing contradictory or unknown elements, it often helps to deepen characterization by portraying your characters as more complex.

For example, my short story "Spoils of War" is a Civil War tale about a ten-year boy and his mother who walk to a federal prison camp in Missouri. It is told in first person, through the eyes of the little boy, and the character of the mother was to me the most interesting thing about the story. But the reason for the mother's most significant action at the climax of the story remains a mystery to me.

Here's the situation: After having sex with the provost marshal general in order to obtain her husband's release, the 26-year-old mother discovers that her husband has died of his wounds while in jail. But she keeps silent when his body is carried out past her, and instead pretends that one of the remaining prisoners – who is scheduled for execution the next day – is her husband. So she and the boy leave with him.

What kind of person would have the guts to do this, I asked myself after the story was finished. Was it a courageous act, or was it disrespectful to the memory of her husband? Did she want to save at least one man from the firing squad, or was she so pragmatic that she knew her odds of survival were better with a man around?

Characterization, of course, is a tremendously complex subject that book upon book has been written about. But if you remember a few things as you are starting to write, it is unlikely that you will go far wrong: show, don't tell; understand your characters well enough to know what they will do in just about any situation; and when they surprise you, let them run with it.

Research

Western fans are particularly sophisticated when it comes to history. It's not enough simply to get the dates right, but you must make the entire story as *authentic* as possible. That means getting the details right as well.

A novelist has an obligation to get things rights. For me, nothing destroys an author's credibility more than a glaring anachronism, such as having cartridge revolvers in the hands of Civil War soldiers. I'm not claiming that I don't make any mistakes – I do, and people sometimes let me know about it – but I do my best. When my attention is called to a mistake, and if it is an unarguable fact, I make a note to correct future editions.

Western readers are especially knowledgeable about firearms. If there is one area where you have to be careful, this is it. For example, if you have a cartridge revolver in the Civil War, it had better be a foreign make or you're going to get called on it. Although there were American-made rifles that accepted cartridges during that period, there were no domestic cartridge handguns because of a protracted patent battle taking place. All American-made revolvers were of the older cap-and-ball type.

Horses are another area where you need to use caution.

I am fortunate enough, having come from a rural background where guns were a part of everyday life, to have a good working knowledge of guns and their history. But I've never been around horses much, and despite doing the requisite research I sweat bullets every time I have to describe a horse in detail. So I ride a little, and read a lot, and try to deepen my understanding.

To do good research, you must be willing to admit what you don't know. You must adopt what is called the "beginner's mind," to free yourself of preconceptions and expectations. Otherwise, your research will be a frustrating and lifeless affair.

Unfortunately, people nowadays are notoriously reluctant to confess their ignorance. I'm not sure if it's because question-asking seems impolite, or whether folks are too self-conscious to draw attention to themselves. Most likely, it's a lack of basic communication skills. Having taught freshman composition, I know that college students are particularly stricken – it seems most would rather sit in stoney and anonymous silence than raise their hands to ask the teacher to clarify a particularly difficult concept. For them, learning is a passive experience, as if they were mere vessels waiting to be filled with enough facts to pass the course. This reluctance to admit what we don't know – driven, perhaps, by fear or the pressure to appear learned – is a major obstacle to real learning.

Begin by assuming that you know absolutely nothing about the subject. Start with a broad look at the time period and location you intend to write about. The library is still the best place for this, and if you are lucky enough to be near a major metropolitan or university library, count your blessings. Don't confine yourself only to books, but investigate newspaper and magazine indexes as well. Most libraries now have their general card catalogs on computer, which will make the search quicker and more accurate – providing you take the time to learn how.

Take notes. Photocopy only those things you find supremely useful, such as maps or illustrations, because the tendency is to leave large blocks of copy unread. Organize your research. When I began research for *The Sixth Rider*, I bought a five-ring spiral notebook for notes on place names, personalities, history, and slang of the period. I also made a month-by-month chronology, from the year 1850 to the turn of the century, leaving plenty of room for entries. This helped me to double-check sources and to recognize patterns and relationships that otherwise would have gone unnoticed. It also provided a quick reference when I needed to check a date, an age, or a name.

Keep a journal of the books you have read on the subject. In addition to basic bibliographic information, record what you found helpful or annoying about the book. Good indexes are particularly useful, as are extensive bibliographies. Note the call number if it's a library book, so that you can find it again if you need to.

Cultivate a relationship with your local librarians, They have ways of locating books and articles that are beyond the reach of mere mortals. Also haunt your used bookstores, because used books are not only a bargain, but many of the titles you're after are probably long out of print.

Obtain maps and photographs of the period. When I was researching the Dalton raid, for instance, I found the fire protection maps that were produced every few years for the insurance companies were particularly helpful; for Coffeyville, I found maps which gave the names and locations of all the businesses in the town plaza, where the action took place.

One of the hardest things to find out is what daily life was like during a certain period. For this, your best sources are the journals, diaries, and letters that have been left behind by those who were *there*. Many historical societies index this type of material, so it is not difficult to find.

Finally, don't hesitate to be creative in your research. If it all possible, visit the location you are writing about. Prowl around and ask questions. When I was preparing to write *Sons of Fire*, for instance, I spent some time in Cass County, Missouri. While there, I noted a sign put up by the Missouri Conservation Department proclaiming a particular location as the "Amarugia Wildlife Area." I had never heard of Amarugia before, even though I thought I was familiar with all of the local place-names, so I wrote the state conservation department about it. Believe it or not, they said, the area was named for a sort of backwoods kingdom that a trapper named Owens set up in the 1830s. Court was held every Saturday night, with fines for trespassers amounting to a gallon or two of cider. Later, this wild area became a hiding place for outlaws and was rumored to be the domain of ghosts and witches. Incredibly, the kingdom – ruled over by descendants of Owens – remained until well into the Twentieth Century.

This stuff was too good to pass up, so I placed Amarugia in the book, and now a lot of people think I'm kidding when I tell them that Amarugia is real. But this sort of thing – lucky coincidences that provide just the thing you need – happens all the time in my research. I don't know how to explain it, and many other writers have told me it happens to them as well. It may be synchronicity or positive thinking or just plain magic, but whatever it is, if you are serious about your research it will eventually happen to you. Take it as a sign that you're on the right path.

When do you know you have enough research?

You won't. No matter how much work you do, when you sit down to write your story, there will be some detail or a nagging question that you still need answered. There is also a sense of security in research, instead of the stark terror that often seizes writers when confronted with a blank page or that mocking blink of a cursor on the computer screen. But at some point, you have to call an end to research and begin to write.

That point is usually when you have the structure of your story laid out and most of the obvious historical questions are answered. Don't wait until your every single question has been answered. Begin now, while the research is fresh and you can still recall your original enthusiasm for the story.

Writing

The actual writing is the most mysterious part of the fiction process, and it is also the most difficult to explain, You probably have heard about how much discipline it takes to write, how you should keep regular hours, keep track of your progress, and so forth. I'm sure many writers have found that advice helpful, but it has never worked for me.

My stories require a certain amount of gestation, time that my subconscious mind works things out while my conscious mind does research. If I try to force a story before my subconscious is ready to give it up the writing is invariably flat. Nothing seems to work, and I find myself reworking the same passages, over and over, but to no satisfaction.

But when my subconscious is ready, things tend to go quickly and almost effortlessly, The story tumbles out. I go into a kind of trance, a kind of waking dream, in which I vividly imagine characters and events. Although it took me a couple of years of research before I was ready to write *The Sixth Rider*, when I was finally ready the novel was finished in six weeks.

Often, when I read a page from a story I've written years or even months before, I am shocked – I don't remember writing it.

This is a very different process than writing nonfiction. I spent ten years in daily journalism before devoting myself to fiction, and while writing newspaper stories I've never experienced this dream-like trance. Rather, my mind was always occupied with down-to-earth things like fact checking, caption writing, and deadlines. Except for some techniques used in feature stories, there really is no comparison – it's apples and oranges. I was once asked to identify the major difference between investigative reporting and writing fiction. The only reasonable answer I could think of was that, so far, nobody had threatened to kill me over the fiction. But it is early.

Also, it is possible to tell Greater Truths – more important, long-lasting truths about the human condition – through fiction than through journalism. Journalism is important, very important, although lately many reporters have become as lazy and pack-minded as those they cover.

Although I tend to write in creative bursts, then let my batteries recharge for a while, many other writers succeed by steady production. By writing a little bit, each and every day, they accumulate a substantial body of work in a year's time. The smart money is on the latter approach.

And it doesn't matter if you write on a computer or with a No. 2 pencil on yellow legal pad. Use whatever it is that makes you feel the most comfortable.

Don't stop your writing to check a fact, unless it is something of absolutely crucial importance. Instead, make a note of it and come back to it later. Don't break your flow by looking up a word in a dictionary. There is plenty of time for that later. Do not make the mistake, however, of letting a spell checker on your computer do all the work for you. These are fine for catching typos, but cannot recognize differences in word meanings. You may have *their* for *there* and so forth.

Don't agonize over grammar. As long as you are reasonably competent in the language, with consistent tense and good noun-verb agreement, you'll do fine. The only grammar book you really need is *The Elements of Style*, by Strunk and White. In this little book you will find easy-to-understand answers to all but the toughest grammar questions. If you have a grammar problem that is not addressed in the book, then your writing is probably overly complex.

Let your ear, and not a textbook, be your final authority on matters of grammar. This is why reading your work aloud can be so helpful. Take the prohibition about splitting infinitives. This rule has been around for six hundred years and nobody really remembers why we are not supposed to do it. But there are items when an infinitive positively *must* be split in order to achieve the correct emphasis. "To boldly go where no one has gone before," say the captains of the Starship Enterprise. "To go boldly" is weak and needlessly stiff in comparison.

While you are writing, remind yourself often that you are composing a story, not a history lesson. Resist the urge to show off your research. Keep the footnotes to yourself. If a fact does nothing to advance the story, then throw it out. Your focus should always be on story and characterization.

William Goldman said it best, when introducing his screenplay *Butch Cassidy and the Sundance Kid*. He had researched the story for about eight years before he finally put it down on paper. He got Butch, and Sundance, and Etta *right*. Even when Goldman veered from what is strictly the truth about this trio, he was telling a greater, human truth.

"Not that it matters," Goldman said, "but most of what follows is true."

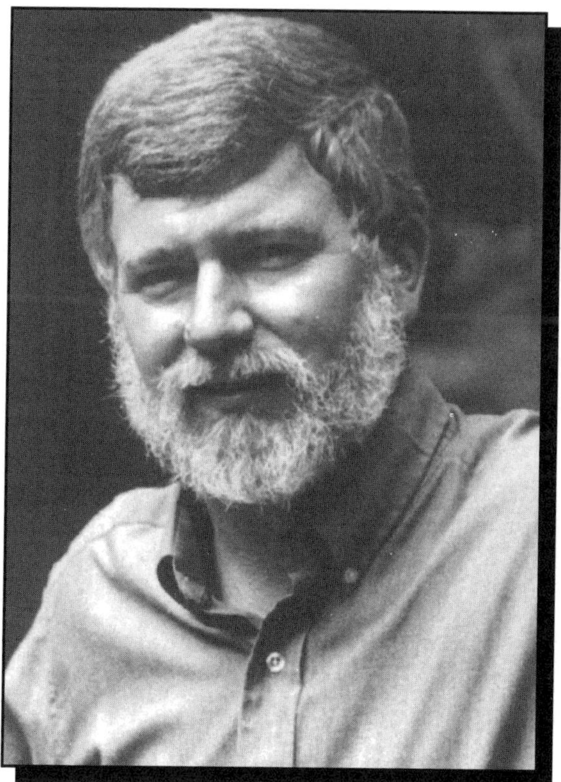

Jim Hamilton

Editor of the *Buffalo Reflex* since 1978, Jim Hamilton has guided the newspaper to numerous state and national awards. He has twice been named the state's best weekly newspaper columnist in the Missouri Press Association's competition, and has twice earned second in National Newspaper Association competition.

A collection of his newspaper columns entitled *River of Used To Be: Reflections of an Ozarks Editor*, was published in 1994 by Seven Oaks Publishing Company and is currently in its second printing.

Hamilton is the past president of the Ozark Writers League and is also involved in other writers' organizations.

A native of Dallas County, Missouri, he currently lives with his daughter, Melissa, on a small acreage near Buffalo, Missouri.

Writing the Personal Column:
Only Strangers Come to the Front Door

Only strangers come to the front door of our house.

Folks who know us come around back and holler through the kitchen screen. We recognize their voices, ask 'em in to sit a spell and share a pot of coffee.

Like trusted friends, successful personal columnists find the way to their reader's back door, too.

While starched-collar essayists vainly pound with profound prose at the front, the personal columnist gains invitation in with a soft, familiar knock at his reader's favored portal, where the screen is pooched like a kangaroo's pouch, paint around the knob nicked by fingernails, and the window smudged by children's hands and noses.

He comes through the same door as sacks of groceries and kids home from school. It's the door flung wide to welcome a son home from the Army, the door slammed shut with a rattling of glass when lovers clash, a corner of its curtain pushed tearfully aside as the pickup rips gravel from the drive, the door left unlocked for the prodigal's return.

It's the writer's door to the reader's house, the latch lifted by shared lives.

It's a door opened by familiar experiences:

> . . . roses, with spindly, stickery vines that reach out and grab Dad's overalls as he walks past them to the truck.

It's a door opened by familiar sensations, sounds and pictures:

> Winter fell on us Sunday like a chill wind through a sweaty T-shirt. . . Birdshot pellets rattled lightly in the hours before light. Monday morning found car tops iced with a crunchy white frosting and random snowflakes drifting like lost feathers after a pillow fight.

It's a door with scars our fingers have traced:

> Once chalk-white and smooth as the face of a child, the old markers are broken, weathered and rough to the touch of the palm, wrinkled and spotted like the hands of an old man. . .

Each of us has to discover our own path to the reader's door, engage his trust and friendship with prose. We must discover our personal style and technique.

The personal essay (it becomes a column when it's published as one) is often an emotional response to an experience. It's an attempt to attach a verbal handle to a mood or feeling.

This excerpt from "The Smell of Sawdust" is an example of that kind of effort:

> Citified and civilized, I was as a man shot dead but not yet fallen, walking among the strange faces and voices of others unliving.
>
> Until I returned to the woods, and was there

> revived by the chut-chut of the chain saw, the sweet smell of oak sawdust, the rough feel of bark on my fingers, and the sharp crack of wood busting under my splitting maul.
>
> Alone in the deep dark oak woods, I returned, as I must every fall, to the roots of my raising, put my hands on the axe handle, felt the pure sweat of woodcutting soak my stocking cap, and reveled in the poetry of each swing of my axe.

Writing is both craft and art. Just as the artist knows his canvas, his paints and his brushes, the writer should know the elements of his craft. His use of those elements transforms the craft into art. Given the same canvas, colors and brushes, no two artists will create the same picture.

Even if not always conscious of them, effective writers follow rules to maintain a clear and consistent focus on their topics. English teachers often require a thesis statement. You don't have to state if, but you do have to know what it is, and stick to it.

STRUCTURE: A good personal essay has a distinct beginning, middle and end. Easy enough. Plenty easy to leave out one of the three, too.

In the whimsical "Missive to a Trout," I begin simply: "It is not a good day to be a trout."

The next 500 words support that thesis with such elaborations as:

> Better you were anything today but a hatchery trout, for you have been fostered, fed, fattened, freed and deceived, all for the cause of sport.

The close reflects the premise stated in the opening:

> Show but the wiles of a fingerling, and you will quickly become a fillet. . . Truly, it is not a good day to be a trout.

Adopting a more serious tone, the metaphorical Christmas time "Journey" adheres to the same structure. It begins simply: "The Christmas tree is history."

The metaphor of that action is suggested in a succeeding passage:

> I chucked the holiday out the door a day ahead of the tree. I'll be just as quick to shuttle Ninety-Four on its way too.

The body of the essay reveals why:

> On the morning of September 30, her hand slipped quietly from mine as she was overtaken by the cancer which had pursued her for two years.

The last paragraphs then echo both the beginning and the gist of the essay:

> I've tossed the Christmas tree in the yard, and I'm about to do the same with Nineteen-Hundred and Ninety-Four . . . This is a new journey.

Simple examples. That's the point, especially if you're a novice – keep it simple.

The most effective writing chases the subject along a well-defined path. It's like a trip down an old Ozarks highway. Stay between the ditches, and watch those side roads. They may be scenic, but it's easy to get lost in the woods and never get back to where you started. Stick to the highway – don't overlook the potential for new destinations down untried roads – but always bring the reader back home.

THE FIRST KEYSTROKE: The first paragraph is the most difficult to write. Some folks never get past it. Nothing is so intimidating as a blank sheet of paper or computer screen.

The first word is a hurdle we all have to leap, even after hundreds of columns. The first paragraph stalls green news reporters, and it can mire any of us at any time for the same reason – we want it to be perfect. We worry that our first words won't be brilliant. Journalism students are encouraged to write "snappy" leads, which spawns some truly awful first sentences to otherwise well-written news stories, or intimidates writers to the point that they finally give up and head for the coffee pot.

The cure for stymied starts? Write. Don't worry if it's not Pulitzer material. Just write it. Get past that first line and tell the story.

GRAMMAR: Rules of rhetoric shouldn't be ignored, but they ought to be guideposts, rather than trees felled across your path.

There is a time for writing and a time for editing. If you have something to say, just say it. Sit down to the keyboard and write it. Don't even think about writing a "personal essay." Tell your story as if you were telling it to your friends over coffee. Then edit. You may find little is needed.

WHAT TO WRITE: The personal essay allows for a lot of latitude. You can write about almost anything. Getting it published is another matter. What you write will probably depend on what you can sell. That will depend on your personal style, particular expertise, and what the editor wants.

The field of personal columnists includes all kinds, from Mike Royko writing about Slats Grobnik and the Chicago Cubs, to Baxter Black and his wry perspectives on the comedies of cowboy life. But, newspapers and magazines rarely carry two of the same. You can learn what the market wants and write for it, or write what you want and hope to find it a home. Try the first option, if you can live with it.

WRITING TO THE SENSES: Personal columns, like

compelling fiction, should appeal to the senses, as well as the intellect.

What columnists are really trying to do when writing of emotions or experiences is get in touch with the similar experiences or emotions of readers.

That's done, at least in part, by painting familiar images, such as these from an unfinished essay:

> Outside my bedroom window a sheet of tin covers the woodpile. When it rains, the gutter drips on it in an incessant melody. It's not the real thing, but it's close to the sound of rain on the roof of my folks' old barn, the soothing music of spring.

Word pictures. Imagery as much as anything can convey a sense of who we are as Ozarkers. Metaphor and simile provide concrete images to interpret the abstract, to illustrate the extraordinary features of the most ordinary.

The example is from "Red Rusted Bucket Season":

> Sunday morning saw the season's first skiff of ice on a puddle on the porch. The hayfield out front was flocked in ermine white, while foxtails in the fence row bristled like delicate crystals. . .
>
> . . . A brown and black wooly worm crosses the porch, his coat the color of fall. Coffee steams from my just-filled cup, like the early morning haze.
>
> Through whiskers the color of frost, I take a sip, watch the wooly worm crawl, and contemplate the arrival of fall-that red rusted-bucket-brown season of naked limbs and blazing trees.

That is the gist of the personal column as I write it – experience and emotion shared in a voice familiar to readers.

It's my path to the back door. Every writer has to find his own.